Library of
Davidson College

*Environmental Damage
and Control in Canada*

4
People Pollution

Canadian Society
of Zoologists

*Environmental Damage
and Control in Canada*
M. J. Dunbar, GENERAL EDITOR

1. **Environment and Good Sense**
   M. J. Dunbar
2. **A Citizen's Guide To Air Pollution**
   David V. Bates
3. **Freshwater Pollution, Canadian Style**
   P. A. Larkin
4. **People Pollution**
   Milton M. R. Freeman

Milton M. R. Freeman

PEOPLE POLLUTION

Sociologic and
Ecologic Viewpoints
on the Prevalence
of People

SPONSORED BY THE CANADIAN SOCIETY OF ZOOLOGISTS
McGILL-QUEEN'S UNIVERSITY PRESS
MONTREAL AND LONDON
1974

301.32
F855p

© McGill-Queen's University Press 1974
ISBN 0 7735 0195 9 cloth; ISBN 0 7735 0207 6 paper
Library of Congress Catalog Card No. 73 94315
Legal Deposit Second Quarter 1974
Printed in Canada

77-5287

This book has been published with the help of a grant from the Social Science Research Council of Canada using funds provided by the Canada Council.

CONTENTS

PREFACE	vii
1. Introduction	1
2. Current Trends in Canadian Development	8
3. Canada in Relation to Global Productivity	31
4. The Population Issue in Canada	60
5. Canadian Population: The Roots of the Problem	90
6. Population Policy and Normative Behaviour	110
7. Future Directions: Rationalizing the Issue	136
EPILOGUE	150
REFERENCES	155
ADDENDUM	169
INDEX	177

PREFACE

In a demographic sense whereas it is true that the future of the present is in the past, it is equally true that the future of the future is in the present. Hence, if man seeks to understand and thus control his destiny on Earth, therein lies one powerful reason for advocating constant exposure to the results of population studies. I hope that this brief text will make clear that a fundamental relationship exists between population-related phenomena and the environmental problems that we, in common with many others, experience in daily life.

It is a safe prediction that in Canada in the next two or three years the media will convey expressions of a growing national concern about population-related issues. Though the output of demographic research findings is enormous (but not in Canada), the references used in this book have been selected where possible to reflect basic issues that will probably continue to be debated or will form the necessary substrate for such debates in future.* Thus, however unacceptable my reasoning or conclusions are to some, now or in the future, I hope that the extensive bibliography will serve as a useful reference source for orienting the concerned reader's search for pertinent information.

Clearly I am indebted to many scholars for the contributions their studies have made to my own understanding of the field. Perhaps it is natural that as an ecologist I should study population behaviour, but my residence in the Northwest Territories and in Newfoundland (both areas of very high human fertility)

---

* An Addendum has been added (August 1973) drawing the reader's attention to recent Canadian publications appearing after the manuscript of this book was completed.

served to focus not only my attention, but also my concern, on the ramifications of this behaviour. One person, more than any other, has been influential in directing my professional interest to this field of inquiry: Dr. Mary Douglas, of London University, some years ago gently but persuasively moved my thoughts toward the anthropological study of populations.

I would also acknowledge my gratitude to the forbearance shown by many others during my sometimes desperate but always hectic attempts to meet self-imposed deadlines: Mrs. Shirley Fraize, who ensured that the speedy typing of early drafts of the manuscript was completed, at the Institute of Social and Economic Research, Memorial University of Newfoundland, and Mrs. Elizabeth Burghoorn, who undertook similar responsibilities at McMaster University. My wife has throughout provided not only support and patience during the writing, but invaluable research support during fieldwork. I am indebted to the Killam Awards Programme of Canada Council for financial support of this work.

I am grateful for the permission of Mr. Robert Graves to reprint the poem "In Broken Images" from his book *Collected Poems 1965.*

Every effort has been made to check for errors, and any that remain are the sole responsibility of the author.

November 1972   MILTON M. R. FREEMAN

chapter one

INTRODUCTION

We are burdensome to the world. The elements scarcely suffice us. Our needs press. There are complaints among all. For now nature will not support us.

TERTULLIAN (Second century A.D.)

*Our stability is but balance and conduct lies
In masterful administration of the unforeseen.*

ROBERT BRIDGES (1930)

We must take a new look at the problem. We must stop thinking in terms of a race between production and reproduction, a race that can never be won. We must realize that our aim is not mere quantity, whether of people or goods or anything else, but quality—quality of human beings and the lives they lead.

JULIAN HUXLEY (1963)

It is becoming apparent that if current trends continue, the future of life on earth could be endangered.

UNITED NATIONS (1969)

Economic development is the process by which the evil day is brought closer when everything will be gone.

KENNETH BOULDING (1970)

We can cheat on morals. We can cheat on politics. We can deceive ourselves with dreams and myths. [But] to act without rapacity, to use knowledge with wisdom, to respect interdependence, to operate without hubris and greed, are not simply moral imperatives. They are an accurate scientific description of the means of survival.

BARBARA WARD (Stockholm, 1972)

It seems an inescapable conclusion from reading a small sampling of the plethora of reports, releases, expert prognostications, and opinions on the subject that the world, and obviously every sovereign state within it, faces not just one crisis but a multiplicity of interrelated crises. Some, such as the ideological confrontations raising the spectre of a nuclear holocaust which a decade ago seemed to overshadow all else, have subsided or stalemated to the point where we now feel almost confident that national and international institutions can handle any remaining problems in this area of difficulty. The contemporary problem is more difficult, because, among other factors, some of our best friends—indeed even ourselves—are the bad guys. It is not our determination to preserve and enhance—at any cost—our supreme affluence that threatens to precipitate collective international suicide, but, ironically, it is the by-product of this seemingly assured affluence itself which now threatens to engulf us all.

Growth of population, of urbanization, and of industrial production, all formerly respectable indices and objectives of the good life, now subject whole societies to acute levels of social, economic, psychological, and aesthetic stress. There can be no consolation for Canadians, or anyone else, derived from the observation that we are all in the same boat, nor from the academic proposition that some are further in the mess than others; if I may borrow an acid quip from Dr. Paul Ehrlich: "There is no point going steerage when you book passage on the Titanic."

Given the widespread and deep concern of many Canadians toward these problems, why yet another book on pollution, on the environmental crisis? Leaving aside any narrow, personal motives that stimulate a person to write a book, there is a more important reason. I will attempt to justify that decision by sidestepping to another question some readers may have: why the title *People Pollution*? Certainly I intended no irreverent or facetious pun, though I admit my choice of title was to provoke attention. Every writer hopes his work may become known, most undoubtedly hope it may be read with pleasure and profit. Furthermore, when that book is written with the intention of contributing to some issue of social import, a primary task is to help facilitate people's rethinking of their existing knowledge on the subject, to make new linkages among the inventory of facts they have already accumulated. If the writer can help cause this strengthened understanding and awareness to metamorphose into the conviction and determination to act, then his job is that much more rewarded, for as the sociologist Emile Durkheim has rhetorically asked: "Why strive for knowledge of reality if this knowledge cannot serve us in life?" To return to the title of this book: did I mean people as pollutants, or people as causers of pollution, or that in the present environmental crisis people and pollution share some ecologic equivalence? It really doesn't matter which is the most appropriate interpretation. What *does* matter, however, is that the reasons behind my decision to provoke become clear, even if the intended meaning of the title itself remains uncertain.

Pollution, like dirt, results from misplaced matter; resources in fact, but occuring in inappropriate amounts and in the wrong location. The injurious characteristic of pollutants derives from the affront they present to the system of which they are part. Some offend more than others, and herein lies one major obstacle to overcoming the increasing threat pollution poses, for some pollutants at this time bother little more than the aesthetic sensibilities of a small fraction of the population. Given that pollutants run the gamut from the mostly harmless discarded cigarette package through the mildly offensive odour and gaseous effluvia of burning garbage to the invisible but insidious mutagenic emanations from atomic-powered generating stations, where does one draw the line? When does the pollutant present in subclinical doses, produced as a side-effect of a possibly beneficial process, or the potential pollutant similarly produced, become offensive, dangerous, anathema?

A great deal of our present interest in pollution stems from a subjective concern with the quality of life. This is not to deny that there is in fact objective damage to ourselves and our environment caused by many pollutants present in our air, water, and urban and rural surroundings, but merely to stress that our cultural values as well as our individual physiology and scientific tests help identify and define pollution. Thus a junked automobile in a blighted urban area may offend or outrage the passing suburbanite, but to a generation of neighbourhood children it represents a valued resource, a vehicle perhaps for escape to more enchanted and rewarding surroundings than real life provides for them. A similar piece of scrap may, on the edge of a prairie or at the bottom of a lake, increase the availability of animal habitats and thus enhance ecologic productivity, diversity, and stability, but to the picnicker or underwater swimmer it remains, by any other name, just junk.

The subjective nature of the problem then gives justification for including social and cultural considerations in any analysis of the environmental crisis in contemporary Canada.

Yet another reason for drawing attention to environmental problems from a perspective not usually associated with the normal orbit of science and technology is that the choices and decisions increasingly required are of an ethical nature, and ethics—some evolutionists' views notwithstanding—are culturally determined. The crux of the ethical dilemma is contained in the statement made recently by physicist Harold Gershinowitz (1972: 383) in the pages of *Science*: "Rarely is a problem the result of wanton, irresponsible action. . . . No one deliberately sets out to make waste. What is annoying or hazardous to some people results from an action or process that benefits or is convenient to someone else."

It therefore becomes necessary, somewhere along the line, to make decisions in the interest of or beneficial to a majority of people alive today or even to generations not yet born; nevertheless some choices will be considered by some segments of our present society to be unacceptable infringements on viewpoints or freedoms whose exercise they consider their birthright.

Such problems, related to the environmental crisis complex, will be considered in this present book. Another, and less philosophical, reason for extending the discussion into the realm of sociology and the humanities is the following: basic to an understanding of the crisis that besets people who live as we Canadians do is the fact that the partaking of and the sustaining of this very lifestyle cause the pollution and allied problems that threaten to overcome us; therefore, quite simply, the more of us there are, the greater the threat. Although, as Canadians, we are seemingly so few and enjoy the riches of a large, generously endowed land, we must rationalize our population–resources equation if we are to persist on our own terms. Indeed, the only thing our relatively small population and large area buy us is time: time to prepare the necessary adjustments that must be made, not just by government but by the majority of free thinking, morally and politically responsible citizens.

The time is long past when Canadians could take comfort from the increasingly irrelevant statistics presented in geography texts and the Canada Yearbook; as we consume so we pollute, as we export so we contribute to others' pollution of the global ecosystem we all share. We are all in this together, and it behooves us to "get with it," to join the commonwealth of nations now seriously questioning various of their domestic and international policies on the broader canvas of longer-term persistence and benefit rather than merely short-term profit. As Professor Dunbar pointed out in the introductory volume of this series, we must recognize the error and futility of we/they dichotomies, for indeed we *are* all in the same situation together (Dunbar 1971: 7). There is no truth in the once comforting myth that a sparsely populated Canada represents little threat to the global ecosystem, or indeed to anyone, whereas populous industrial countries such as the United States, or populous less-developed countries such as India, are the only ones who impose ecologic or geopolitical stresses. In ecologic terms, 22 million Canadians probably represent a drain on world resources equivalent through their high level of consumption to that of 400 million Indians; and this same 22 million at our standard of living generate as much pollution as would 1 billion Indians. So, indeed, Canada and India *are* unequal, but not in the reassuring manner many of us might imagine.

Furthermore, Canada claims a significant role in international development; our aim is to help raise living standards (and hence consumption) in the less-developed countries of the Third World. Even if we helped India to come half-way to North American standards, in itself an admirable objective, we will have, incidentally, brought the equivalent of another United States to the world community. It is well to remember that North America, with only 6 per cent of the present world population, consumes about one-half the world's resources each year, and it has been estimated that, if increases in population and production in the United States continue as at present, this one country will require virtually 100 per cent of the world's production of resources by the year 2000. Such a situation is clearly impossible, but surely indicative of a disquieting trend nonetheless (unless the United States, ourselves, and others modify greatly the present consumerism ethic), for among many other problems we cannot ignore are the probable pressures that will be exerted by such growth-oriented industrial countries on those territories and sovereign states wherein lie the assets needed to fuel their competing industrial juggernauts. Canada, as both an exporter and domestic consumer of these required resources, is in a double bind: the threat to her own environment is that posed not only by her present and future population but by the many hundreds of millions of consumers in this hemisphere and elsewhere whose future existence and prosperity, and ours as a trading partner, will increasingly depend on the fresh water, power production, minerals, forests, and other resources of this land.

This book will explore from a cultural–ecologic perspective certain dimensions of the population–environment complex of interactions. Although any comprehensive discussion on the population issue as it relates to social policy must concern itself with various demographic parameters, for example population distribution and immigration, this essay is deliberately, and restrictively, eclectic in its treatment of the topic. Rather than attempt in such a small volume to treat all aspects, I have especially focused upon one of the more basic and vexatious population questions, namely human fertility. This is not to deny the pertinence and importance of other aspects of the Canadian population issue, but I have felt that a degree of focus is a necessity to illustrate the complexity of the problems.

Some readers may question my use of the term 'ecologic' in the title and elsewhere in the text. Ecologic to me refers not only to matters pertaining to the relationships existing between a population of living organisms and their environment, but embraces a particular way of looking at problems. It is the ecologic perspective that I wish to stress, meaning a holistic, integrative, and multi-disciplinary approach to stating and, hopefully, understanding a problem. Indeed, the one thing which ecologists of differing disciplinary backgrounds do have in common is a shared conceptual approach to problem-solving and an overriding interest in understanding the process of adaptation *sensu lato* (see also Holdren and Ehrlich 1971: 1-2).

Earlier I said we have time on our side, but how much time? And time to do what? What are our options if we are to remain in control of the consumption whose consequences may eventually threaten the integrity of the body we call Canada? It seems clear that there is only one sequence of purposive behaviour to follow: we must reach a thorough understanding of the nexus of problems that besets us; we must then decide rationally what can be done about such questions in general; and then decide whether we are prepared to behave in similar, adaptive, fashion; and lastly, we must transform our good intentions into immediate resolute action.

chapter two

CURRENT TRENDS IN CANADIAN DEVELOPMENT

Population numbers can cause a variety of stresses to a system of which they are part. Considering merely pollution effects, and taking a local view, the population may grow at a faster rate than do the physical amenities required to prevent massive pollution problems. An example here is the current inability of most large urban centres of Canada to expand adequate sewage-disposal facilities at a rate even equivalent to their local growth of population.

Alternatively, and again from the local point of view, population growth may be slight, or otherwise not itself an immediate cause for alarm, but the absolute number of people in the area may be so large that increasing difficulty is experienced, both physically and economically, in continuing to provide adequate services. An example here is the disposal of solid waste once proximate disposal sites become used up or volume becomes so great, for example, as to overcome the natural ability of the region to neutralize contamination of ground water.

Thirdly, and of course ultimately, the overall population of very large areas may become so great that local numbers are all but irrelevant due to the overriding problems of overspill from adjacent, or even distant, areas of gross population size and pollution-generating activities.

Canada at various points today suffers from all three classes of population problems. An appreciation of demographic trends and projections will show how much more acute the resulting threats will probably become until they are insoluble, make life unlivable, or cause us to take remedial action.

URBANIZATION

There are many environmental issues associated with the urban scene: noise, noxious emissions, and physical congestion caused by road transportation, problems attendant upon providing essential services to a high-density human population, the often slow-to-change displeasing physical appearance of certain large sections of towns and cities. The solutions sometimes appear all but unobtainable, but, given the will and the financial resources, there is little doubt that the imagination and technical skill of Canadians could overcome these stumbling blocks if high enough national priority is accorded to them. Such cautious optimism, however, appears somewhat less warranted when the social dimensions of urban problems are considered: the increasing lack of social responsibility toward the amenity and property rights of others, crimes of violence, mounting despair brought on by poverty and the increasing impersonalization of the individual at the hands of "the authorities," and other well-known social disorders apparently manifested with disproportionately greater frequency the larger the urban centre.

These problems of the city and the rapid growth of urban populations are far from being restricted to Canada, of course, for the accelerating movement of people to the cities has been a world-wide phenomenon for the past fifty years at least. It has been estimated that by the year 2000 the urban population of the world will have increased twentyfold over the 1920 count, whereas world population will have quadrupled in the same period of time.

In Canada the urban growth phenomenon was slower to start than in the United States or Europe, but since the end of World War II Canada's rate of urbanization has been greater than that of any other developed nation: 4.1 per cent per annum, compared with 2.7 per cent of the second-ranking country (the United States). Indeed, almost the total population increase occurring in this country between 1951 and 1966 was absorbed by the growth of our cities and towns.

This trend is almost certain to continue: by the year 2000 the size of our urban population will be more than double today's total. Urbanization in Canada will involve not only continuing movement from the rural areas to towns and cities but also, as is characteristic of the contemporary world-wide urbanization process, movement of residents from many smaller to fewer, larger, urban centres. Thus we will see an intensification of the pattern observed between 1961 and 1966 when Canadian cities with populations in excess of 100,000 grew at twice the rate of smaller towns and cities.

Such rapid growth can remain controlled, benign, and, indeed, beneficial if the challenge it presents is met. Failure to overcome the potential problems combined with such growth heralds a nightmarish prospect of a cancerous Canadian heartland with pockets of decline and decay distributed from the Atlantic to the Pacific.

Some predictions of the future distribution of population are available: planners expect that by 2000 half the people in Canada will be living in nine cities each having a population of one million or more, and that fully one-third of all Canadians will be in the three megalopolitan areas of Montreal, Toronto, and Vancouver. The Montreal–Toronto population, however, would probably form part of a huge interlocking urban system stretching from Windsor to Quebec City and containing almost half of Canada's 34 million people. Incidentally, this particular population concentration does not represent the total stress imposed on the life-support system of the region it occupies: just across the St. Lawrence River and bordering ailing Lake Erie and Lake Ontario will probably live a further 59 million people in an urban corridor stretching from Detroit to Rochester!

How do Canadians react to these expectations, I wonder? Do we have sufficient faith in policy-makers and planners at various levels of government to welcome the prospects, or do we merely assume, perhaps rather naïvely, that life will not be much different then for, after all, we *are* rational beings. If one looks for reassurance, then it would be as well to avoid polling the many disadvantaged citizens resident in all large Canadian cities today, those who find living conditions almost or actually unbearable and the attitudes and inactions of the civil authorities equally intolerable.

Pollution Probe investigators at the University of Western Ontario conducted a survey to determine the degree of congruence between the views of the citizens of London, Ontario, on the one hand and of the officials in City Hall on the other, concerning the projected future size of their city. According to the city planning office, London's population will grow to 300,000 people in a decade, a prospect considered desirable by only 28 per cent of citizens polled. Furthermore, the 1980 projected population of 400,000 was acceptable to only 10 per cent of current residents. Nevertheless, the "Proposed Official Plan 1970–1990" for the city states that its "optimum population" lies between 500,000 and 750,000 and that this goal will be reached in about thirty years. It is pertinent to ask how these planners define the word "optimum." It appears from the poll taken that values and feelings of the citizenry have either no weight or very low currency in the planners' scale of criteria. An alternative conclusion is that the objectionable consequences of urban growth, explicitly stated by the Londoners as pollution, traffic congestion, crime, crowding, civil unrest, and increasing noise levels will be overcome by that city's urban developers. Yet another alternative exists, and one that has serious implications for us all if true: namely, that the planners share the misgivings of the citizenry but are resigned to the apparent inevitability of continued growth and will attempt to cross the various bridges of misfortune as they come to them. A good philosophy for the terminal cancer patient perhaps, but what a tragic way to go, especially when, as in this instance, there might still be time to seek a cure for the underlying malaise.

HOUSING

Even allowing that Canada as a nation can boast some of the most enviable statistics regarding housing standards, a crisis does exist across the nation and, given a high rate of population growth, poses an almost insoluble problem. Currently there are about 200,000 fewer housing units than families in Canada and an additional 165,000 new family formations take place annually. Added to this equation are the half-million substandard housing units needing replacement. Statistics such as these give the reader little awareness of the mounting human costs involved through the failure to provide such a basic necessity as decent and adequate housing, more especially since this misfortune is not indiscriminately suffered but appears to represent unnecessarily cruel and unjust indifference toward the poor and disadvantaged by more privileged members of their own society. Writing of the steady streams of Canadians who leave the economic depression of the rural areas to seek their fortunes in the cities, a federal government report states:

> Here [in the city] too, is poverty in its rawest and ugliest form. No pretty gardens or painted cottages here to camouflage economic depression. Poverty in the worst areas of the city core is abundantly visible in the decrepid structures which form its housing, the cracked pavement of the streets which are its recreational area, and the rodents which are its wildlife. . . . Its residents are not simply families struggling to catch up to the average national income; too often they are people fighting to retain a vestige of human dignity and self-respect. (*Report* of the Federal Task Force on Housing and Urban Development 1969: 11.)

This same report goes on to stress the urgency of the problem if Canada is to avoid the deterioration of its national life that has overtaken those other nations who provided, too little and too late, the help their urban citizens required when attempting to participate in one of man's most novel and recent major experiments, namely, mass coexistence in the metropolitan setting. The remainder of this chapter will explore some of the implications of increased growth of the urban environment in Canada.

A sad commentary on our values in this age of technological wizardry is that today, in North America, good housing is still a luxury product out of the reach of millions of Canadians and Americans, and that a stubborn gap still persists between the cost of adequate shelter and the amount of personal income.

In the United States it has been estimated that a quarter of the population lives in slum housing, a statistic which certainly suggests that the root of the problem is not wholly technological. In Canada a recent report has noted that federal housing programs have merely helped the more affluent regions of the country to build better (though not more!) houses, but has scarcely assisted the poor regions (Atlantic Development Board 1969: 75) A similar conclusion, that poorer Canadians are not being served by existing housing schemes, appears to have prompted the resignation in April 1969 of the federal Cabinet Minister in charge of housing. At about the same time a front-page story in a leading Canadian newspaper warned that the Toronto housing situation would shortly be chaotic with a long, hot summer of evictions occurring from lower cost rental units (*Globe and Mail,* 25 April 1969).

Reforms in the legislation and regulations governing public and private investment in Canadian housing do not appear to have brightened the prospects since then. The present federal Cabinet Minister in charge of housing admitted that, given the predicted rate of population growth and urban concentration, a solution to national housing problems is far from within reach, and explicitly "given a rate of growth like this is almost impossible to handle" (*Globe and Mail,* 21 May 1971). Readers interested in a thoroughgoing analysis of some causes of North American housing problems are referred to an essay entitled "Housing in the Year 2000" (Abrams 1968: 209–28).

Slums can be taken as a manifestation of a housing shortage. The consequent contribution to the creation and perpetuation of urban immiseration by an expanding population in the absence of an equally vigorous house-construction program is self-evident. But, there is an important cultural, as well as demographic, component to the creation of a housing shortage, and it relates to changing values regarding desirable residential localities.

The growth of cities has involved not only additions of people at the periphery but also an increase in density at the centre. The reason for this increasing density relates to the economic *raison d'être* of the city, the fact that productive activities can be maximized by reducing spatial and communication distance between component parts of the total commercial enterprise. Thus, when labour, financial capital, stocks of raw materials, manufacturing, distributive and marketing facilities are situated at the shortest distance from each other, the commercial process can better realize the goal of greatest production and maximum profit. As a consequence, most major cities grew at some logistically important location, for example a port, where the raw materials could be assembled, population thereby encouraged to settle, and the manufactures and services produced readily distributed to markets outside of the urban centre itself.

The advent of mechanical transport served as a catalyst for an accelerating growth of the cities. Given that in the commercial world non-productive time is in effect money not earned, rapid intra-urban movement became a prerequisite for continued spatial enlargement of these urban centres. It has been estimated, for example, that the advent of the motor vehicle facilitated a twenty-five fold increase in area of land available for development within a given time distance (MacNeill 1971: 71). But this very potent growth agent, in large measure, has been responsible for the increasing social, economic, and physical problems of the metropolitan areas and now contributes increasingly to the demise of the latter as centres of continued growth and prosperity. It is apparent that even though many commercial enterprises can continue to flourish in the intense activity generated within the inner core of the city, this very intensity, creating as it does noise, congestion, pollution, and the physiological stress such conditions exacerbate, precipitates an outmigration of some city residents to more salubrious areas farther from the city centre.

The result of this movement to suburbia is an ever-greater level of activity within the city caused by the increasing numbers of workers now having to traverse urban space by vehicle rather than on foot as was done earlier.

Increased vehicular flow through the city, requiring additional land allotted to roads and, more recently, areas for parking vehicles, ensures that land value remains high because of the competing uses to which it might now be put. A combination of rising costs and loss of desired residential amenities causes further movement of city dwellers to the fringes, where expenses are lower and various environmental characteristics are deemed more desirable.

The continuing growth of the city, and particularly its expanding commercial and industrial functions, increasingly draws potential workers into its orbit; the rural poor, some of whom are displaced by the growth of suburbs, require residence close to their urban place of work. Despite the availability of housing caused by the movement to the suburbs, however, costs are high for both occupancy and maintenance. To meet these high costs, sharing—leading in time to overcrowding—results. The deterioration of neighbourhoods quickly follows from this mode of occupation because, whilst the demand for housing remains high, given the modest level of economic returns from the tenant there is no equal pressure felt by the landlord to maintain the quality of housing. The rate of deterioration of housing quality in congested sectors tends to accelerate, indeed to multiply, the problems of the particular area and leads to a chronic condition known as urban blight. The etiology of this condition is well analysed in an article entitled "Housing Policy and Urban Renewal" (Adamson 1968: 222–39). It remains, however, to reiterate the outcome of this historical process of urban development: poor people come in time to occupy not only less space per person but also the poorer quality housing in neighbourhoods often lacking the amenities now considered necessary by the majority of urban residents. This plight results not just from their lack of disposable income but also from the shortage of alternative improved housing.

There is no doubt, given the size of our national housing problem, that more than a simple accelerating flow of investment will be required if all Canadians are to enjoy the "improvement of housing and living conditions" set as an objective thirty years ago by the National Housing Act. Unfortunately, increasing the flow of funds, either through higher individual earnings or through mortgage and construction capital, does not appear to be the answer. Incomes in metropolitan Toronto are rising at a rate which is as high as practically possible, given the Canadian economic situation, but the housing problem in

Toronto has been intensified rather than ameliorated by this high economic growth rate. One government study has asked: "If the most affluent metropolis in Canada cannot solve its housing problems without special measures, what hope is there for an increase in income alone to be sufficient to solve the Atlantic regions' housing problems?" (Atlantic Development Board 1969: 81). In fact, it seems very probable that raising income in the face of continued high demand for a scarce product can only force the price higher still (as it has in Toronto) and despairingly out of reach of large numbers of people.

Estimates suggest that in the next thirty years Canada will require from 7.2 to 10.1 million new housing units to replace existing substandard dwellings and to house the projected increase of population to 34 million (MacNeill 1971: 78). The economic cost of this expansion will be especially heavy because, by that date, 94 per cent of the Canadian population will likely reside in urban areas, requiring almost a tripling of the area of high-cost serviced land adjacent to these cities. A further important negative aspect of this growth is the loss of a further 3000 to 4000 square miles of farm and recreational land close to existing high-density population areas.

SEWAGE AND WASTE WATER

On the whole, Canadians (especially those living in urban areas) have a remarkably tolerant attitude to living in other people's filth. Residents in some urban centres are seemingly more indifferent to these unsanitary conditions than others but, overall, especially considering the North American cult of body freshness and goal of whiter-than-white laundering, the national record for public hygiene is inexplicably remiss.

In 1967 the nine major urban centres of Canada included about 35 per cent of the total population; yet only one of them claimed to subject 100 per cent of its waste water to treatment. These nine centres produced nearly 850 million gallons of waste water or sewage per day, with the largest single contribution coming from the 2.4 million people in the Montreal area. Montreal's production of 290 million gallons per day included 268 million gallons of untreated effluent, with one-third of the remaining flood treated to the extent that it has about half of the lumps strained out before being dumped into the river. Quebec City, with 42 million gallons of effluvia per day, does not even strain out the lumps, a token performance neglected also at Halifax and St. John's.

Vancouver treats about 41 million gallons of its daily total of 100 million gallons; cities such as Ottawa, Hamilton, Calgary, and Winnipeg claim to treat 100 per cent of their effluent, but this merely consists of homogenizing the soup and allowing some of the constituents to settle out. By this process, known as primary treatment, about 40–60 per cent of the solids are removed, but the pollution-causing suspended nutrients and certain toxic substances are freely discharged into the rivers and lakes that serve as our continental vascular system.

Edmonton and Toronto are the only major centres in Canada where the treatment of waste water goes one step further. Toronto claims that all its outpouring of 194 million gallons per day is subjected to secondary treatment, whereas Edmonton asserts that about 20 million of the 37.5 million gallon daily total is so treated. In secondary treatment, bacteria are allowed to attack the organic nutrients and other compounds, so that after a period of holding a relatively clear effluent having only 5–10 per cent solid content is discharged. Unfortunately, this effluent still contains up to 80 per cent of the inorganic nutrients that form the major food of organisms causing eutrophication, or aging, and ultimate death of many of our continental freshwater bodies that serve as collection sumps for this enriched waste water.

Thus far the description pertains only to the major urban areas of Canada. Overall, more than 40 per cent of all Canadians have no municipal sewage system at all, though regional disparities cause this figure to rise to 90 per cent of the population in the Maritimes and in Quebec.

Of all the provinces Ontario appears to have the best control over waste water, with more than 90 per cent of the provincial population served by some kind of sewage-treatment facility. But even here none of the treatment goes beyond secondary processing and only 59 per cent of the total treated goes that far. Half of all domestic sewer lines are connected to storm sewers so that periodic overloading, during rain storms or spring thaw for example, result on those occasions in inefficient or no treatment of domestic sewage. According to a report published by Pollution Probe researchers at the University of Toronto, the provincial Minister of Energy and Resources admitted that many treatment plants in the province were grossly inefficient and overloaded (Chant 1970: 59). The secondary plant at Cobourg, for example, was found to discharge the sewage after ten minutes' processing; the operation should have taken up to nine days!

If solution of the problem appears difficult now, it will be that much more pressing and awesome if left neglected. Sewage just does not go away on its own and the size and venom of the beast increases with time. It is a fact that the most widespread source of both degradable and non-degradable liquid pollutants is domestic sewage. To be sure, a pulp and paper mill or another type of large chemical industry can produce an enormous pollution potential, equivalent to that generated by an urban area, but such enterprises occur in scattered locations, thus producing local, though devastating, environmental effects.

Thus, given that domestic sources of potential pollution are widespread and tend to include a broad range of possible pollutants, two additional factors conspire to make the future environmental threat that much more demanding of attention now. Firstly, the consumption of domestic water, which currently stands at about 125 gallons per urban resident per day, is rising at a rate which suggests a demand of between 300 and 350 gallons per capita per day by the year 2000. Secondly, the continuing shift to urban living suggests that by 2000 about 94 per cent of all Canadians will be in such centres (compared to only 74 per cent in 1967); that is, 32 million out of 34 million Canadians will be consuming larger quantities of water and discharging equal amounts of waste water that requires treatment of some sort.

Because of the enormous backlog of installations required to cope with the present problems of waste-water disposal, the estimated cost of providing the needed services now amounts to $100 million annually for capital costs and $48–$60 million per annum for maintenance and operation (MacNeill 1971: 102). At the present rate of progress, which is far below that required, it has been estimated that by 2000, when further procrastination *will* be impossible, the annual cost for installation of plant will be between $240 and $380 million per annum with corresponding operation and maintenance costs of $550–$674 million per annum (MacNeill 1971: 105). Large as those estimates appear now, however, it seems highly probable that, given the present abuse of our water resources, those that do remain will be so valued in the year 2000 that the primary and secondary treatment facilities listed above will be considered quite unsatisfactory and as a consequence even more expensive tertiary treatment plants will be mandatory.

SOLID WASTE

At the present time each Canadian generates about 1600 pounds of solid waste a year; the trend is, of course, upward, so that by the year 2000 each person will probably produce 7.5 pounds daily compared with the present 4.5 pounds. In thirty years' time, then, Canada's estimated yearly production of solid waste will amount to 930 million pounds, in contrast to the comparatively trifling 36 million pounds of garbage produced annually now.

Present disposal methods are coming under increasing attack, and, strange as it may seem in this day of space technology, garbage is disposed of in the same fashion as it was in grandfather's day: it is simply buried or burned. Burning, however, creates air pollution as well as requiring a physical plant that local governments seem to loath to install merely to handle garbage. Thus the practice of dumping has remained a popular option, being cheap, convenient, and relatively safe.

Today, however, middle-class people are moving to the suburban developments proliferating on the outskirts of most towns and cities; thus the formerly proximate town dumps must be moved further out, causing proportionately increasing costs for garbage disposal. Also, because of the huge volume of solid waste urban areas presently generate, simple landfill operations can result in ground-water pollution hazards unless sites are carefully chosen and proper precautions taken. Such operations, moreover, are likely to remain in use for some time, for studies have indicated that under existing technology it is generally uneconomical to install incinerators for population concentrations of less than 55,000 people (MacNeill 1971:98; see also Morgan 1970, for a good discussion of Canada's garbage problems).

RECREATION

Recreation implies a meaningful use of leisure. Leisure is important to us because of its intimate relationship to re-creation and hence the continuing ability of the individual to remain creative and alive: all work and no play indeed not only make Jack a dull boy but impair his adaptiveness to the point of chronic social and physical disadvantage.

According to one writer, leisure is not to be confused with mere filling-in of free time with banalities, for in the creative cycle, work and leisure complement each other:

> In work there is a focusing, a contraction of faculties and an acuteness of consciousness. During leisure, there is an unfocusing, a relaxation of faculties, a greater diffusion of consciousness. . . . With this relaxation, the field of consciousness widens to include what previously had been peripheral, subconscious, and suddenly, great unifying patterns are recognized and the great "inductive leap" occurs. Herein we have one valid explanation of why, throughout the ages, man's imperishable intuitions have come during his moments of leisure. (Martin 1964: 28.)

If one subscribes to this interpretation of the positive value of leisure, then the increasing need of it by members of a society such as our own is readily apparent. Firstly, in most jobs today there is a humdrum sameness, born of the machine age, and as demanding on the human psyche as it is unfulfilling. The urge to "get away from it all" is in all of us, but more so in the average town-dweller—for obvious reasons.

The Canadian population, as we have already observed, is becoming urbanized to a greater extent each year; added to this are our increasing affluence and rising sophistication (born of greater education and exposure to informational media and social opportunities), both additive functions tending to increase the desire and means of consuming in recreation. In Canada the use of parks, both national and provincial, is doubling each five years, and recent estimates place our immediate needs at between forty and sixty new parks during the present decade. Some of these projected new parks should be wilderness, but it must be remembered that nearly 90 per cent of Canadians' leisure time is spent in the community of residence (MacNeill 1971: 82). The implication is that a great increase in municipal parks is required, especially in the heavily built-up areas where, unfortunately, competing land use causes the cost of setting aside acreage for recreation to generate some very difficult political decisions. MacNeill (1971) estimates that the present 20,000 acres of municipal parkland in Canada's six largest cities will have to be increased more than five-fold in the next thirty years to provide a standard only half as good as that recommended for urban residents by the U.S. National Recreation Association.

Stewart Udall, while U.S. Secretary of the Interior, observed that it is possible to double-deck roads and even cities, as land becomes scarce or very valuable, but it remains impossible to double-deck parks. And for those who believe that multiple housing, including high-rise complexes, will provide the means of releasing urban acreage for recreational use, it is only fair to say that such a style of urban living has generated a series of problems unlikely to be solved by the mere provision of more recreational facilities. One commentator has observed:

> In one area of Metropolitan Toronto, where there is a good deal of Ontario Housing Corporation highrise, there has been a 76% increase in delinquency, a 50% increase in illegitimate births, a 400% increase in children seen by the Children's Aid Society; in one school in that area, with 800 students, 200 are in urgent need of psychiatric services. Very few of them will get it. Very few of the babies born under the choking frustrating conditions in multiple housing units cannot be described as "high risk" babies, psychologically so mutilated that they are the living dead. (Callwood 1969: 68; see also Cappon 1971.)

As nineteenth-century political economist John Stuart Mill observed, a population may be too crowded, even though all have a roof over their head, clothes on their backs, and food in their stomachs. Furthermore, he notes, and few would disagree, being able to retreat from the press of humanity is not only beneficial to the individual but a condition which society could ill do without.

TRANSPORTATION

Expanding transportation facilities not only are indispensable for maintaining our present high-quality material existence but collectively pose a serious challenge to all Canadians if the overall quality of national life is not to deteriorate in the future.

The automobile holds a key place in discussions on urban and interurban transportation requirements, not only because of its proximity and ubiquity but also because it stands at centre stage in the contest between man's desire to enjoy maximum individual convenience and pleasure, on the one hand, and his refusal to act with self-restraint to prolong the exercise of that enjoyment, on the other. To be specific, I need only remind the reader of the overwhelming challenge to resource-conserving and pollution-minimizing public transportation systems posed by the privately owned and operated automobile. Yet how many of us, myself included, are willing to forego daily the luxury and convenience of driving to work or play in order to use the bus or train? It is this insistence on individual use of automobiles that frustrates the authorities in their efforts to improve the quality of the service of public transportation systems, an inability which makes the private use of the automobile that much more frequent and, apparently, justified.

It has been observed that whilst the automobile has brought great benefit to modern society, the costs to man and his environment have been tremendous. The use of automobiles generates a variety of forms of pollution—air, visual, audio, and land — and these combined, especially at strategic locations at the periphery of the metropolitan areas, often create situations where the environment appears completely submerged to the demands of the tin god and its slaves. We have all experienced, at the edge of town, the visual onslaught of filling station vying with filling station, car-wash facilities, muffler services, tire outlets, beflagged used-car lots, new models resplendent on billboards or high-lighted on pedestals, nose-to-tail congestion on multilane highways now increasingly climbing over each other to ensure that the polluted skyline rises even higher into view. Within the urban areas the automobile needs only a modest amount of land to move around in, but it nevertheless uses a considerably greater area to exist in. It has been estimated, for example, that in thirty years' time metropolitan Toronto and Montreal will require two and one-quarter million parking spaces, consuming a total of more than one-eighth of all the land foreseen for the growth of these two regions (Blumenfeld, quoted in MacNeill 1971: 74). MacNeill (1971) further details the considerable costs of this rapaciousness on the part of the automobile.

Two other aspects of the disamenities provided by transportation requirements are air and noise pollution. As people periodically decide to escape the urban areas of residence and employment to enjoy the change provided by the surrounding countryside, so the increased incidence of noise and air pollution contributed by their means of transportation threatens to destroy the greatest amenity and recreational aspects of their new locale, namely, the absence of man-made noise, visual, and air pollution.

Let us consider noise pollution. It has been reported that at 70 decibels of noise the body's autonomic nervous system reacts to the stress: blood pressure and heart rate increase, muscles tense, pupils dilate, and gastric-juice production becomes reduced. At levels above 85 decibels hearing loss begins to occur. A lawnmower motor produces over 100 decibels, as does a moderately powerful motorcycle, whereas a jet plane at take-off generates 130 decibels. Pain is experienced at around 120 decibels; thus, although no pain is experienced from the 70 decibels' background din of a relatively quiet city street, the body is nevertheless subject to physiological stress. Sustained exposure to loud noises produces permanent damage: scientists at McGill University recently reported that more than 80 per cent of adult male Eskimos in one arctic community had significantly impaired hearing, an occupational disability doubtless exacerbated by prolonged use of excessively noisy motorized toboggans. Although the clatter of machines in the once overpoweringly silent

Arctic is very dramatic and obvious, no less of an intrusion and a threat to health is the now high level of background noise the average urban dweller tolerates. Background noise levels in North America have doubled in the last twenty years, and now double every ten years. Indeed, the problems associated with noise have become so acute that some scientists believe noise levels rising, unless abated, at the rate of one decibel per year will effectively and eventually produce a stone-deaf population by the year 2000! (Bailey 1969.)

Very few Canadian cities enact or enforce noise-pollution standards in the same way that they control other activities potentially hazardous to public health or safety (see L. K. Smith 1970). They do, however, recognize the potential danger of air pollution generated by the internal combustion engine. Studies have indicated that exposure to 30 parts per million (ppm) of carbon monoxide gas will measurably impair vision and psychomotor functions. In city traffic carbon monoxide concentrations frequently rise above 30 ppm; some American examples in 1966, obtained during commuter runs into downtown areas, were as follows: Baltimore 24 ppm, Chicago 32, Cincinnati 29, Denver 34, Los Angeles 40, New York 32, Phoenix 38. During briefer periods of maximum exposure these values peaked to 92, 91, 96, 96, 111, 91, and 105 for the seven cities, respectively. The author of a companion volume in this series points out that, as far as carbon monoxide is concerned, although heavy cigarette smoking is far more damaging *to those who smoke* than is the polluted air they breathe (Bates 1972: 19), even those not directly responsible for generating carbon monoxide breathe it in. In metropolitan Toronto, for example, about one million tons of the gas enter the air each year, at some cost to those who breathe the city air.

In a recent study entitled *Only People Pollute,* a scientist has tabulated the individual contributions to total national pollution made by an "average" Canadian family of four (his own, in fact); the modest family use (19 gallons of gasoline a week, average) of a late model automobile accounted for nearly 16 per cent of their total pollution production, or about 10 short tons, together with about 48.5 short tons of air consumed by the car in a year (Mitchell 1971: Table 1). When assessing the demand that Canadians place on the environment, the population density of the urban areas is more pertinent a statistic to keep in mind than the 5.5 persons per square mile for Canada as a whole. Because of our persistent urge to crowd into cities and our increasing dependence on the automobile to make urban life more attractive, population densities of 8,000 per square mile in metropolitan Toronto and of 13,500 in metropolitan Montreal assume urgent significance, more especially since the number of automobiles, presently less than a third that of the inhabitants, grows at a faster rate that do the people of this nation.

GROSS NATIONAL PRODUCT—RECONSIDERED

In 1966, according to data published by the International Bank for Reconstruction and Development, the per capita Gross National Product (G.N.P.) in North America was nearly three times higher than in Europe, nine times higher than in Latin America, eighteen times higher than in Asia, and an immodest twenty-three times higher than in Africa.

Among individual countries per capita G.N.P. in the United States was about $3500, compared with around $2250 for the next three most affluent countries, namely, Sweden, Switzerland, and Canada. Sweden and Switzerland, it should be noted, had a per capita G.N.P. far above the average for industrial Europe ($1230). One-third of the total world population is found in six populous countries (mainland China is excluded because of a lack of economic data): the Soviet Union (with a per capita G.N.P. $890), Japan ($860), India ($160), Indonesia ($150), Pakistan ($90), and Nigeria ($80). There evidently is little correlation between population size and G.N.P.

All projections indicate that not only will G.N.P. in North America continue to grow, but the rate at which it expands will be greater than the rate experienced in the less-developed countries; and, incidentally, it will increasingly become a factor in preventing the have-not nations from becoming more nearly affluent themselves (see, for example, Ehrlich and Ehrlich 1970, Holdren and Ehrlich 1971, for ecological perspectives on the international development dilemma). In Canada, per capita share of the G.N.P. will likely triple by the year 2000, so that

Canadians will dispose of around $7,800 per person compared with the $4,600 per person in most other industrialized countries and $325 in the less-developed world (Kahn and Weiner 1967).

Before we get collectively carried away in a haze of euphoria, however, it is advisable to seek the implications of increasing economic expansion and, indeed, what the full meaning of G.N.P. entails. One conclusion must be made perfectly clear at the very beginning: G.N.P. is a blind or neutral measure of gross economic growth which in no way distinguishes between the beneficial and the downright damaging, the significantly meaningful and the trivial, the lasting and the ephemeral. Thus the millions spent on producing and stockpiling some noxious agent for "national defence" enter into the addition as do similar millions expended on bulding improved health, education, and housing facilities, or the annual re-tooling of a factory to produce this year's soon-to-be-obsolete automobiles.

Clearly G.N.P. in no way measures national well-being any more than growth for its own sake invariably leads to all-positive good. A comprehensive constitutional study prepared for the Canadian government has warned that a major component of increased economic growth in this country will stem from expansion of presently pollution-intensive industries and from activities that presently ravage the environment. The report goes on to state that in fact the forecast growth is likely to occur only if the negative effects of such growth-promoting activity can be overcome. Failure to control and reduce these negative effects will cause us to advance nationally more slowly than predicted, or, if we nevertheless contrive to maintain growth, then it will be achieved until such time as total destruction of the environment occurs. The inevitable conclusion is reached that "it is unlikely that civilization as we know it will reach the turn of the century if current trends are simply allowed to continue" (MacNeill 1971: 33). It is little wonder that economist Kenneth Boulding has suggested that we substitute the term Gross National Cost for G.N.P. (Boulding 1970: 161).

Some will argue that surely government will see to it that such growth as takes place is both regulated and necessary. Up to a point this is very likely, but the administration is called upon to report progress every five years or sooner, and the criteria by which it tends to be judged are not always the most far-seeing and enlightened. This is not to exonerate the state from its sometimes unpardonable lapses; among the biggest contenders for all-time honours in environmental irresponsibility are such government agencies as the U.S. Atomic Energy Commission and the U.S. Corps of Engineers. When their schemes include releasing tidal and shock waves and increasing background levels of radiation, flooding the Grand Canyon (to see if it can be done?), flooding the Yukon Flats and the Everglades, and so on and so on, it is evident we have a problem on our collective hands as co-tenants of continental North America (see, for example, Ehrenfeld 1970: 30 *ff*; and Dunbar 1971, for some Canadian equivalents).

The majority of oil companies and strip miners are perhaps equally unconcerned about the environmental effects of their activities, which they attempt to justify on the grounds that there is a market, or anticipated future market, for their product. The Canadian government has been getting into the act itself by becoming a major shareholder in a consortium of arctic oil seekers. Thus our major bulwark against potential environmental damage over a large part of our national landmass has, to say the least, precipitated a major conflict of interests. It will be of utmost significance to see which interest, protectionist or profiteer, gives way; given the magnitude of the costs and potential benefits, it is hard to see how we can have our cake and not try to eat it too! Thus in 1970 the Canadian government helped maintain interest in the shares of its arctic oil company by facilitating a second promotional cruise of the super-tanker *Manhattan* through the summer pack-ice. Incidentally, that same year the *Manhattan*'s owners were being sued by the U.S. Justice Department for 150 separate offences against federal anti-pollution laws in respect to offshore oil operations (Toronto *Globe and Mail,* 14 November 1970). The stakes in oil are high, as are the dangers to the marine and arctic environment attendant upon its exploitation (see, for example, Ramsey 1969, Weedon and Klein 1971, for pertinent ecological viewpoints).

The problem presented to government, industry, and society is one of economics and ethics in the broadest sence of those terms. Economist Boulding has argued that our present economic theories and commercial ethics may be inappropriate to a system having finite capital resources; only now, however, because technology has pushed us to the limits of that finiteness, are the startling inadequacies of existing economic systems becoming apparent. He asks: Is production and consumption more important than maintaining an optimal stock of capital assets at minimum cost? He makes the telling analogy between the "cowboy economy" with its attendant frontier mentality (which we collectively manifest today) and the "spaceman economy" with its stringent cost-accounting and prudent book-balancing (Boulding 1966).

Boulding's seminal writings, though unorthodox to economists, nevertheless have a familiar ring to theorists in ecology and cybernetics who recognize the adaptive value of increasing a system's stability and hence its long-term viability by building up capital accumulation through reduced energy turnover or flow rates.

Others (for example, Galbraith 1964, Mishan 1969, Lekachman 1971) have drawn attention to the increasing irrelevance of G.N.P. as a true reflection of where society is, and whether it is increasingly "better off" with increased G.N.P. In a thoughtful article entitled "What G.N.P. Doesn't Tell Us," one author calls for the calculation of a Gross National Disproduct. As examples, he cites the billions of dollars spent annually on cigarettes and cigarette promotion, without deficit accounting of the national costs of increased lung cancer and other respiratory ills caused by this product. Similarly, the billions spent on purchasing and operation of automobiles do not take into account the large costs in terms of deaths and injuries caused, air pollution, junked wrecks littering the countryside, and so on (Berle 1968).

The Prime Minister of Canada expressed the following progressive sentiments at a political meeting in Vancouver in May 1971:

> There is no shortage of persons who rationalize that for the benefit of shareholders or taxpayers, raw waste and sewage can be dumped with impunity into rivers or vented into the atmosphere. In the absence of a philosophy of this age we must give the appearance of a generation gone mad. . . . Surely we are not so ignorant as to assume that, somehow, the earth will begin producing more resources at an inexhaustible rate. Surely we do not prefer to live

beside garbage dumps, to breathe smog, and to look out on polluted oceans. Do we really believe that a high standard of living involves daily traffic jams and ear-splitting noise levels? Are we totally indifferent to the world in which our children and grandchildren will be forced to live? Have we, in short, permitted our commonsense and our value system both to be so distorted that we equate "good" with "consumption" and "quality" with "growth." In the name of economic growth, in the pursuit of comfort and pleasure, we have increased the demands upon our environment, and posed new risks and new costs which are often far in excess of the value of the growth or the benefit of the comfort . . . we have been deluding ourselves for a quarter of a century with a misleading bookkeeping system that permits industry, government, agriculture—every segment of the community—to pass on certain costs to society at large. No businessman would calculate his net gain without first taking into effect the deterioration of his plant building, the depreciation of his machinery, and the depletion of his stock of raw materials. Why, then, do western governments continue to worship at the temple of Gross National Product? . . . Shouldn't we, in short, be replacing our reliance on G.N.P. with a much more revealing figure—a new statistic which might be called Net Social Benefit? (Toronto *Globe and Mail,* 31 May 1971.)

We *must* be ever aware of the inevitable costs incurred by increased national production. Gross National Cost, Gross National Disproduct, Net Social Benefit, Gross National Service, or Net Benefit Criterion are all pertinent measures for current development processes overtaking technologically advanced societies. It appears almost inescapable, given continuation of current trends, that environmental destruction, international disharmony, and human dissatisfaction will be the correlates of the increasing transformation of raw materials into consumer items and the invariably unequal distribution of these items among world and national populations. Gaps between haves and have-nots *are* broadening, and aspirations universally continue their runaway upward spiral.

In summary then, we must view the prospect of our increasing G.N.P. with circumspection for, though it stands for material "progress," it has been amply documented that "it is not a measure of the degree of freedom of the people of the nation. It is not a measure of the health of the population. It is not a measure of the state of depletion of resources. It is not a measure of the stability of the environmental systems upon which life depends. It is not a measure of security from the threat of war. It is not, in sum, a comprehensive measure of the *quality* of life" (Ehrlich and Ehrlich 1970: 280).

chapter three

CANADA IN RELATION TO GLOBAL PRODUCTIVITY

There is an increasing number of books and technical reports written by scientists predicting food crises in the not-too-distant future. Authors such as Georg Borgstrom (1967, 1969), Paul Ehrlich (1968, 1970), and the Paddock brothers (1964, 1967) have been among the more compelling advocates. But there have been scientists in other fields (for example, nutritionist Jean Mayer 1964, biologist Barry Commoner 1967, or economist H. J. Barnett 1971), who concentrate attention on other limiting conditions, thus diverting attention from, or at least qualifying, the critical population–food equation. At one time there was a vocal extreme fringe, composed mostly of Marxist thinkers and conservative Catholics, who could not see the problem for the people; the Marxists have since modified their position, leaving Colin Clark (1967) as one of the last remaining ideological supremacists, dedicated to the position that progressive reform of production techniques will ensure man's indefinite future survival.

It is necessary to look at some of these viewpoints, because Canada has the reputation of being a food-exporting nation, and because progressively increasing exploitation of international resources (such as commercial stocks of Pacific and Atlantic fish) directly affects important areas of our national economy, and has even more important effects on regional economies.

First, however, the global dimensions of the world food situation.

Consider that 2.4 billion people in the world are undernourished, malnourished, or otherwise trying to live on inadequate diets, and that 10 to 20 million people will this year starve to death or die of the consequences of this insufficiency of food;

Consider the additional fact that despite heroic agronomic efforts such as the Green Revolution, the gap between world food supply and world food requirements continues to widen;

Consider the dismal statistic that, despite more than 2 billion hungry people in the world today we cannot feed, at current rates of population increase there will probably be 600 million more mouths to feed in 1980 and 1000 million more by 1985;

Consider, then, the injustice of the fact that currently less than one-third of the world population consumes about two-thirds of the food production;

Consider the absurdity of the situation wherein the net flow of protein is from the hungry nations to the well-fed nations;

Consider the morality of the situation where about half the world supply of marine protein is fed to animals in the already well-fed countries.

In asking that the reader consider these global problems, I am being true to the ecological nature of this present inquiry. Since chemist Justus Liebig introduced his notion of limiting factors in the 1840s, scientists have increasingly understood that the viability or functioning of natural systems will be dependent upon the continued availability of *every* essential component above a certain, limiting, amount.

Various component resources required for the continual functioning of our industrial society are clearly in danger of being depleted to the point of effective exhaustion, for there is just so much crude oil, copper, lead, and silver, for example, present in the earth's crust, and these few essential minerals I have mentioned are all forecast to be exhausted within fifty years (Cloud 1968). But the experts anticipate escape from this particular bind, through recycling, reducing consumption, increased development of synthetics, and improvement in means of recovering the minerals from the earth's crust and the oceans.

Some experts are similarly confident that the crisis in feeding mankind can be solved. The sort of food we and others like to eat however, may not be so amenable to indefinite expansion as will be the industrial chemists' increasing perspicacity in overcoming certain other material shortages. If presented with the situation, people could live with fewer automobiles, TV sets, and beauty aids, but today, and increasingly in the future, failure to increase availability of certain nutrients for about half the people alive in the world represents an effective death sentence.

An honest and determined search for the solution of Canadian environmental problems must take place upon the global stage, for it is there that the future of Canada will be ordained. Perhaps the only spur which will move us to seek to preserve our present fortunate circumstances is a true accounting of the costs involved, and the price to others as well as to ourselves and our dependents of not acting prudently whilst time allows.

It was an Oxford University botanist, Professor F. F. Blackman, who earlier this century extended Justus Liebig's understanding of limiting factors to the realization that maximum, as well as minimum, conditions are dangerous to the continued functioning of a biological system. His writings serve as an appropriate antidote to a human tendency to factor out the more obvious and proximate causes of any problem, whilst for present convenience ignoring the presence or significance of the several less evident effective causes. In 1905 Professor Blackman wrote, with respect to understanding certain biological relationships, "This desirable end often cannot be really accomplished without taking deliberate thought to other factors, lest surreptitiously one of them and not the factor under investigation becomes the real limiting factor to an increase in functional activity."

The functional interrelationships linking the Canadian population to others using common resources and global living space therefore appears germane to a full accounting of the place of

Canadians within their environment, an environment which in ecologic, economic, political, and moral terms does not end at the limits of the physical territory known as Canada.

AN EXAMPLE FROM THE LESS-DEVELOPED WORLD

The world's second most populous nation consisting of one-seventh of the current human population, India, with 550 million people will have a projected population of one billion by the end of this century. About one million new Indians are born each month, and annually about 4 million Indian children under the age of 14 years die from the effects of malnutrition (Rao 1969: 134).

To improve the dietary standard of such an enormous population growing at a high rate presents a staggering task. A report prepared by the U.S. Department of Agriculture calculated that if India, in 1963, had distributed its total annual supply of foodstuffs at a subminimal level of 2300 calories per day, 48 million Indians would have been left with absolutely no food whatsoever. More recently, the U.S. President's Science Advisory Committee Panel on World Food Supply has estimated that India's calorie requirements will double between 1965 and 1985, and an ever greater proportionate increase will be needed to overcome essential protein deficiencies (Norton–Taylor 1966).

India's demand for food over the period 1966–71 went up 20 per cent, yet under the Five Year Plan covering that interval only 2 per cent more land was to be brought under cultivation. Evidently great reliance is placed on the use of chemical fertilizers, but this strategy allows no easy solution. Even if one omits attention to the economic costs involved and merely concentrates on the logistics of the problem of fertilizer supply, if India aspired to the level of intensive European agricultural production through application of fertilizers, such a decision would commit about half the world's current annual output of such products (Ehrlich and Ehrlich 1970: 96). In fact, to meet the need for increased agricultural production, India is endeavouring to build plants to manufacture chemical fertilizer; currently, because of various problems, output only reached about 50 per cent of the 1971 target of 2.4 million metric tons. This augers poorly for the future, as Indian agriculture is increasingly pinning its hope for gains on the new high-yield varieties developed as part of the Green Revolution, varieties which require high levels of fertilizer application to thrive.

Fertilizer application is certainly no panacea then; results of at least one agricultural intensification scheme in India show that, despite high levels of fertilizer application, control plots not receiving the benefits of treatment nevertheless equalled crop production in years of good weather (quoted in Ehrlich and Ehrlich 1970: 97). As the Ehrlichs observe, boosting agricultural production evidently requires more than merely supplying fertilizer! (See, for example, Ladejinsky 1970.)

To achieve some of these needed improvements, India embarked on massive Five Year Plans which committed huge quantities of money to agriculture, health, education and training, industrial and other development needs. The expenses and projects are impressive enough, but obviously one must not expect immediate visible advances. It is not just a matter of changing technology or infusing capital, but rather of effecting fundamental alterations in the ways a society transacts its total business, involving changes in customary values, attitudes, and behaviours that have become sanctified by generations of almost invariable use.

Advances are being made, however, even though there must still be further improvements. India produces only about one-quarter the crop of rice per acre that Japan does; there are many reasons to account for this, but certainly one important difference is the heavy reliance of Japanese rice growers on irrigation practices whereas the Indian farmer depends on the monsoon rains alone. Irrigation, though desirable, is costly. Nevertheless, India installed nearly one-quarter million new water pumps and drove 78,000 new wells in 1968–69 to better water her crops. Technology can be improved in other directions too: it is estimated that 10 per cent of India's grain harvest, enough to fill a train 3,000 miles long, is annually destroyed by rats! With a limited, even if seemingly large development budget, nevertheless, to simultaneously attend to so many worthy, but costly, innovative changes is difficult for any government.

So far we have only considered India's mounting food needs in terms of that country's current deficits and rising population (growing at a rate of 2.5 per cent per annum, that is, doubling in twenty-eight years).

But there is another, and often overlooked, cause of increasing consumption or demand for food, namely, a jump in per capita income. It has been demonstrated, by reference to behaviour in individual countries and to fluctuating world demand for various food commodities, that rising levels of per capita income may stimulate a far greater increment in national food consumption than does population increase itself. For example, world grain stocks experienced a sudden reverse in 1961: before that date they had averaged an annual surplus production of about 10 million metric tons, but since 1961 they have averaged a withdrawal from reserves of about 14 million metric tons, indicating a considerably expanded demand over production (Brown 1967: 604).

Thus we must acknowledge not only the effects of an increasing human population in many less-developed nations such as India but also the compounding effect of rising consumption through growth in national productivity and disposable personal income resulting from the industrialization programs currently underway as an invariable part of the development process.

CANADA AND INDIA: POLES APART

Canada is not able to do very much about India's plight directly, that is, by undertaking in some way to feed India's excess population; our annual production of wheat is only about 5 per cent of the world's production. Any continuing presumption that we may have to be "the world's breadbasket" refers to a bygone era when people's numbers and appetites were clearly more limited than today.

We do produce a surplus over our domestic demands; unfortunately for our international trade, the hundreds of millions throughout the world in need of more food do not create any economic demand for the commodity we have for sale, because they are desperately poor, as well as hungry.

Canada has the highest per capita grain consumption in the world, yet individual Canadians actually use, on the average, *less* per capita per year than do Indians. The reason for this apparent anomaly is that grain consumption has two principal components: that eaten directly by people (as flour and cereal products) and that employed indirectly, through use as an animal foodstuff in the poultry, hog, and cattle industries.

Direct consumption of grain increases with a rising per capita income up to a certain level, after which it declines as people become financially able to consume more dairy and meat products. India has not yet reached that threshold, whereas Canada is far beyond it, thus committing much of her grain to animal feeding troughs.

The more significant relationship, in terms of Canada's grain consumption then, is one which associates rising income with an accelerating demand for non-cereal products which nevertheless utilize grain (as an animal foodstuff). Canada has about thirty times the Indian level of per capita animal protein supply and five times the per capita supply of dairy products and evidently needs enormous quantities of grain to maintain this differential status. It has been calculated that each $2.00 gain in per capita annual income creates the need for one additional pound of grain to maintain the high standard of eating (Brown 1967: 604).

Thus, using data supplied by Lester Brown (1967), 22 million Canadians probably consume the same quantity of grain as do 140 million Indians. Using these demand figures another way, we may assume, as many writers do, that absolute world food shortages are bound to overtake the earth's inhabitants before the end of this century; thus, in any final population–food equation, Canada's high rate of population increase will add the consumption-equivalent of an additional one-quarter of a million underfed people *each month* to the world total.

EXPORTING CANADIAN KNOW-HOW: A CAUTIONARY TALE

Given Canada's involuntary and inseparable involvement with the global nature of any population-precipitated crisis in food supply during the coming years of this present century, it is pertinent to inquire into the feasibility of increasing food production through extensive modernization of traditional low-yielding agricultural practices, by means of the so-called Green Revolution, or by increased exploitation of the protein resources of the sea. There certainly is a widespread implicit belief among many laymen that such reforms and panaceas are technologically possible and therefore will be instituted in time. There is also considerable skepticism among many scientists that such reforms are either practically possible or socially and politically viable. The day is fast approaching when food surpluses of the agriculturally productive countries will be inadequate to meet even the emergency needs of the underproductive, heavily populated Third World countries, and indeed, many of these less-developed countries are already exporting their desperately needed protein supplies to the affluent industrial countries to gain the currency they urgently need for various development tasks.

The developed nations of the world increasingly see their international role as exporting expertise in the fields of agriculture, health, technology, economic planning, and other appurtenances of Western industrial culture to the less industrially developed nations. In retrospect, a survey of the various early attempts to "develop" these non-Western nations along quasi-Western lines illustrates the appalling naïvety of occidental governments. Exposes such as Lederer and Burdick's fictionalized *The Ugly American* did much to make abundantly clear to many North Americans that the gulf between "our" world and "theirs" cannot be effectively bridged by good intentions and money alone. The very important and very fundamental cultural differences creating the two worlds are the cause of the difficulty experienced by Western "experts" in their efforts to help non-western nations "improve" their agricultural productivity despite the not inconsiderable industrial and scientific resources of the West being made abundantly available.

Anthropologist Marvin Harris of Columbia University in New York has exemplified the cultural mind block endemic among Westerners in his cogent analysis of the Sacred Cow complex of behaviour and ideologies existing in India (Harris 1966). He takes issue with the prevailing Western viewpoint that a Hindu religious proscription, dealing with the unity and sacredness of life, has forbidden slaughter of the cow (the symbol of this particular doctrine), with the result that the country is overrun with non-productive cows whose very existence serves to restrict the efficacy of other productive activities. This Western belief is typified by a 1953 United Nations report by agricultural experts who wrote, "In India, as is well known, cattle numbers exceed economic requirements by any standard."

As so often when Euro-American expertise is brought to bear on non-western societies and cultural practices, the most pertinent standards of judgement—namely, local ones—are not used to evaluate or rationalize the situation being examined. The United Nations report alluded to above makes irrelevant comparison between, for example, milk production in North America and India; milk in India, however, is produced from buffalo and the value of the cow to Indian agriculture is not measured or perceived in terms of milk or meat production. The primary purpose of cows in India is to produce bullocks which are used as the principal form of power, though another valued function is to supply fuel and fertilizer. These last two are crucial considerations (though again, all but irrelevant in the West) since most agriculture in India is directed toward subsistence production and there is limited cash available with which to purchase fertilizer and fuel. Domestic fuel is a daily necessity in India, as the diet is heavily based on cereals which must be cooked to provide nutrient and energy for man.

The fuel equivalent of the cow dung used for that purpose, at no cost to the householders, amounts to 68 million tons of wood or 35 million tons of coal annually (equals half of India's annual coal production). Evaluated in such locally pertinent terms, Harris shows how India has too few, rather than too many, cattle, and that they are ecologically justified. Gandhi stated: "We have use for the cow. That is why it has become religiously incumbent on us to protect it"; his rationale, in these terms, is entirely reasonable.

The moral of this cautionary tale should be that reforms based on the simplistic belief that what has proved "good" for "us" must be equally "good" for "them" is a very dangerous as well as erroneous basis on which to develop programs of international aid. George McRobie, of the International Technology

Group in London, has reminded us (1969) by way of allegory not only that the rich man has great difficulty in understanding the needs of the poor man but also that the poor man is unlikely to be helped by attempting to adopt or emulate the strategies used by the rich man to further his own particular social, economic, and political goals.

THE PROMISE OF CONVENTIONAL AGRICULTURE

No energy transfer is 100 per cent efficient; this is even more true in ecology than in engineering, so that the amount of living material synthesized at successive stages along a "food-chain" becomes progressively and markedly less.

An oversimplified rule-of-thumb is that about 10 per cent of the food ingested is actually built into the bodies of animals feeding on plants or other animals; actually this level of growth efficiency varies considerably according to the species and the age of the individual, and ranges from 4 to about 60 per cent. Assuming that 10 per cent only of the caloric value of the food ingested is converted into animal protein implies that about 90 per cent of the energy content of food eaten is required for other bodily functions, such as activity, maintenance, and reproduction. Evidently, then, a diet high in animal protein is "extravagant" in terms of environmental resources: land that could support a vegetable crop capable of direct ingestion by man is necessarily required to provide foodstuffs for an animal that eventually makes available only about 10 per cent of that crop for human ingestion.

In point of fact, however, intensive agriculture and modern animal husbandry do better than the hypothetical 10 per cent ecological efficiency would suggest. It is a truism to say that crops that are calorie-rich are also relatively protein-poor, and as man cannot live by bread alone animals are therefore raised for protein rather than calories. It is also true to say that some of the amino acids essential for sound human nutrition are probably most easily, if not exclusively, available through eating animal protein.

Conversion of plant protein to milk and eggs represents the

most efficient transfer, at about 25 per cent; pork is only about half as productive (14 per cent) and beef and lamb (10 and 8 per cent, respectively) are even less so.

However, the use of ruminants (cattle and sheep, for example) as food producers does have a place in agriculture, for the gut flora of these herbivores allows conversion to usable form of certain plant proteins otherwise unavailable to man.

As mentioned earlier, the efficiency of protein transformation depends not only on species but also on the age of the individual animal. Growth efficiency of young animals is higher than that of older ones. In the broiler industry, for example, young chickens are killed at about three to four months after hatching when their growth efficiency is seven or eight times higher than later in their lives (even though chickens have not yet produced eggs at that early age). The rise of the broiler and hog industries in recent years, the economical price of poultry, and the continuing high price of beef give ample evidence of the differing physiological efficiencies of these various animals.

Many plant crops are high in protein and, being lower down the food chain, would be expected, on theoretical grounds, to provide the best hope of raising the agricultural production of the biosphere to satisfy the needs of the progressively increasing numbers of hungry people, most of whom suffer from protein-deficient diets.

At present, too, we ignore many potential sources of protein; for example, leaf protein is at best fed to domestic animals or used as a fertilizer, but could be processed directly as human food. Biochemist N. W. Pirie, an authority on "unconventional" sources of food, has reported (in Cooke 1970: 39) that sizable amounts of leaf protein were harvested from sugar-beet tops (450 pounds per acre), pea pods and stems (300 pounds), and potato tops (225 pounds). By comparison, an acre of beans yields about 1100 pounds of protein per acre, and a good wheat crop produces about 700 pounds of protein per acre.

At present certain crops are grown especially for their high protein yield: soybeans contain 40 per cent protein, and field beans about 25 per cent. The cost of producing a plant crop is less than that expended to raise animals (whose food has to be either grown or purchased). Thus one cost-benefit analysis established that a pound of soybean protein could be produced for one-thirtieth the cost of one pound of beef protein, and one-eleventh the cost of one pound of poultry protein (Breth, quoted in Cook 1970: 38).

Evidently not only financial cost is incurred if a population aspires to eating a diet high in animal protein: it is also expensive in terms of land. Meat, with the exception of fatty varieties such as pork, does not provide a large share of daily calorie requirements which are usually met by cereals and other starchy foods. Given the high yielding cereals now grown, and the small gains to be foreseen through attempts to increase the efficiency of energy conversion in ecologic networks, it can be expected that a diet high in animal protein will increasingly become a luxury which progressively fewer and fewer people in the world will be able to afford. This luxury status will be especially so for such inefficiently produced commodities as beef and lamb. To produce a North American type of diet requires about eleven times the acreage than for a subsistence diet. If we in Canada are to contribute to the feeding of the seven billion human beings who will be alive in thirty years' time, we would be in a much more favourable position if we (a) adopt new modes of diet, which create less demand for ecologically inefficient foodstuffs, (b) develop new modes of food production, allowing greater productivity under sustained yield conditions from agriculture, fisheries, and perhaps industrial sources, and (c) produce fewer consumers.

Clearly, there is little possibility that we will voluntarily adopt the first course; the second strategy forms the subject of the following pages; the third option will be further discussed later in this book.

Modern agriculture is a relatively recent adventure in terms of the human exploitation of the surface of the Earth: out of 2,000,000 years of cultural man's existence on Earth, more than 99 per cent of the time has been spent as a hunter and a gatherer of wild foods.

The recency of this innovative behaviour should give us reason enough to question the generally presumed ecologic viability of the agricultural enterprise. Such events as the dustbowl era in the United States, the constant advance of many deserts (as typified, for example, by the conversion during the Christian Era of the Roman Empire's North African grainlands to desert and near-desert conditions), and current high dependence on ecologically devastating pesticides and chemical fertilizers constitute well-known results of man's ill-advised agricultural practices which tamper with, ignore, or upset the natural processes of vegetation, climate, and biogeochemical cycles.

But the evolution of agriculture heralded a spectacular breakthrough in man's ability both to meet his daily food requirement and to greatly expand and diversify the cultural and social pattern of his existence. The increase in energy supply that agriculture made available to man resulted from a variety of adaptive strategies; for example, improving the fertility of the soil or changing the nature of the plant cover through the controlled use of fire, or by judicious selection of various appropriate crops and their careful husbandry by weeding, irrigation, and so on.

The importance of some of these strategies, irrigation for example, is that it increases the amount of land available for planting, and allows extension of agriculture to regions otherwise only marginally productive. The extension of agricultural practice to new lands probably has been the most important single factor in allowing the enormous and rapid increase in human population since the Neolithic Period. It has been estimated that at the start of the Neolithic, say 10,000 years ago, there were around 5 million people on Earth. By the beginning of the Christian Era this number had increased to 200–300 million, and by the middle of the nineteenth century the one billion mark had been passed. Even though it took nearly two million years to reach the first billion, it only took eighty years to pass the second billion (in 1930); by 1975 the fourth billion will have been reached. Thus, the 1930 human population will have doubled in size in only forty-five years compared with a doubling time of one million years before the age of agriculture, though it would be absurd to attempt to explain this phenomenal growth merely in terms of increase in food production.

Today, about 10 per cent of the Earth's total land surface supports man's crops, which is a considerable proportion of all land capable of supporting vegetation. Clearly not much increase in acreage can be expected in future years, and in fact a good deal of potentially productive agricultural land is converted to non-agricultural use annually with the growth of urban areas and industrial activity. There are certainly no new lands waiting to be put to contemporary agricultural use, as there were during the period of colonial expansion that heralded the period of fastest growth in human population size, starting in the mid-seventeenth century.

Agricultural practices can change of course: for example, the development of fast-growing short-season crops could push the range of agriculture into the higher latitudes. Very often, however, the economic and social costs of attempting to develop viable agriculture in marginal regions of short growing season and limited off-season employment doom such land projects to early failure. In some examples of extending agriculture across climatic frontiers (as for example, in the Virgin Land Schemes of the U.S.S.R.) soil erosion frequently follows the disruption of the fragile vegetation–soil complex in these semi-arid continental regions (see other examples in Ehrlich and Ehrlich 1970:92).

Recently, however, the development of higher yielding crop varieties has further expanded agricultural production. This improvement has resulted in part from introductions of suitable foreign crops: the potato from South America to Europe, or the soybean from China to North America are two notably successful importations. Further advances in productivity have been the result of selective breeding: for example, high-yielding varieties of rice with a growing season reduced by 20–30 per cent thus allow more crops to be raised under conditions of continuous cultivation. Not only plants, but animals too, have been "improved" by advances in selective breeding: modern breeds of dairy cattle now produce up to 20,000 pounds of milk per year, compared with around 600 pounds per cow in some of the "unimproved" breeds. Egg production is yet another notable example, though in this industry better understanding of poultry physiology and advances in technology, as well as animal genetics, have increased the output fully 1500 per cent over the "unimproved" feral condition. Clearly, however, "improvements" cannot continue indefinitely into the future, and only small positive increments are possible now for most modern breeds.

Today the need for even more intensive agricultural production results from the rapidly growing human population, the expansion of urban–industrial areas at the expense of farmlands, and the endemic under-nutrition that prevails over most of the settled areas of the world. Important technological innovations have contributed to the intensification of production so far achieved; mechanization, irrigation, fertilizer, and biocide development rank among the more noteworthy advances. For example, it has been estimated that when U.S. farms completed large-scale conversion from horses to tractors about 70 million acres of cropland previously required to raise horses could be given over to growing foodstuffs of direct use to man. Mechanization, however, requires huge cash and energy inputs to sustain itself, and often a massive economic and political infrastructure (to bring about price-support schemes needed to keep agri-business operative), so that such reforms are beyond the reach of any but the more highly industrialized countries (see, for example, Griffin 1969, Ehrlich and Ehrlich 1970: 98).

Irrigation, though about 6,000 years old, has yet to reach its full potential as an aid to agricultural production. The fact remains that, not only in the warmer and more arid regions but in the temperate zones too, crop yields can often be greatly expanded by increasing the water available to the plants. Irrigation is a technique fraught with ecological dangers, however, and because fresh water is an increasingly strategic resource on the surface of the Earth it is politically and economically, as well as ecologically, expensive to supply (see, for example, Marine 1970).

One environmental side effect of irrigation that uses the more readily available (and hence cheaper) water in lakes and rivers, for example, is a rise in the water table, thus increasing the likelihood of flooding as well as intensifying the salt content of the soil to the point where the land becomes less, rather than more, productive. These dangers can be overcome by using ground water rather than river water, but the deep drilling required is expensive, and the greatest need for irrigation is often in just those regions of the world where financial resources are particularly scarce.

A further indication of the complex ecologic ramifications of utilizing irrigation for increasing agricultural productivity lies in the field of public health. According to World Health Organization figures, a parasitic blood disease (Schistosomiasis) has now surpassed malaria as the world's number one infectious disease. Schistosomiasis, or bilharzia as it is widely known, is an extremely debilitating and dangerous malady whose causative organism gains entry into the blood stream through the unbroken skin of people standing in infested water. It is estimated that about 250 million people are afflicted by this ailment and, because these victims are mostly agricultural workers, food production suffers in just those areas where the use of irrigation is being increased in an attempt to overcome low agricultural productivity.

Increased water alone will do little to improve crop yields in many marginal areas where nutrients, such as phosphorus, potassium, and nitrogen, are also in limiting amounts in the soil. Historically, the use of fertilizers becomes widespread only after the supply of new land suitable for agriculture has been depleted. Heavy application of fertilizer is therefore a more recent event in North America, compared with its long-time use in Europe or Japan.

The history of improving cereal yield in Britain (as an example of a country using intensive agriculture) illustrates the importance of fertilizer application for increasing productivity. According to data assembled by agricultural scientist Dr. G. W. Cooke (1970), in medieval Britain about 400–500 pounds of wheat were harvested per acre. As a result of new planting methods, this crop had about doubled by the early nineteenth century; by the middle of the nineteenth century a further 25 per cent increase had been realized by rotation of crops, allowing restoration of some soil fertility. Around the time of World War I, some fertilizer was being used and some improved strains were being planted so that further gains were made, harvests averaging 2000 pounds per acre being recorded. Greater use of fertilizer and improved means of weed control caused an additional 10 per cent gain in the inter-war period, and in the decade following World War II intensified use of fertilizer and more new crop varieties gave yields averaging 3000 pounds per acre. During the 1960s, fertilizer levels have been expanded to the maximum possible under existing agricultural conditions: wheat yields today, of around 3500 pounds, are about double those harvested in 1900.

In countries presently practising intensive agriculture, yields will probably not improve through greater application of fertilizer, with the possible exception, on some soils, of crops which would benefit from greater use of nitrogen compounds. As upper limits for nitrogen application are reached, however, a critical situation occurs requiring careful adjustment of quantities added, because inappropriate dressings lead to crop losses (Cooke 1970: 27–28).

It appears unlikely that either potassium or nitrogen fertilizers will be scarce in the immediate future, though phosphorus soon will become less easily obtained and its widespread use in agriculture has a disastrous effect on surrounding bodies of freshwater which become enriched through drainage from the adjacent fertilized farmland. The imminent death of Lake Erie will be a direct result of such flushing of nutrients into waterways, and, given the widespread use of such biologically potent chemicals, there is good cause to agree with Stanford's Dr. Paul Ehrlich when he opines that world agriculture today is an ecological disaster area. Contamination of potable water supplies by drainage from fertilized farmlands has already occurred in parts of the United States, and increased levels of nitrate in supplies of drinking water can be particularly dangerous to small children when converted to nitrites in the digestive tract.

Fertilizers are not the only chemicals that have aided modern agriculture in its efforts to increase food supplies for man and his domestic animals. Evidently the purpose of agriculture is to divert as large as possible a proportion of the potential organic production of the land to man's direct use. Elimination of crop competitors (through weed control) or of those competing with man for the same crop plants (through control of pests and plant pathogens, for example) can facilitate a greater diversion of the crop to man; the recent development of an armoury of synthetic biocides has greatly helped in this task, though at some cost.

The intended, and therefore "good," effects of the use of biocides include, for example, the eradication of some insect pests through insecticide spraying programs. Moreover, this intended action is indivisibly linked with a host of unintended effects, which are also discriminate even if their target is not the reason for the spraying action in the first place. The extermination of the peregrine falcon in eastern Canada and the local disappearance of several species of pelicans, grebes, and other flesh-eating birds are examples of discriminate though unintended effects of DDT applications in agriculture and in public health.

The indiscriminate, unintended effects are even more insidious and dangerous because we know neither the full extent nor the full significance of these events. This situation pertains because biocides are not usually target-specific, even though there usually is some particular organism aimed at in any biocide application program (be it a fungus, bacterium, or noxious invertebrate animal). The effect of such complex chemicals in the ecosystem is to act as ecological simplifiers, for they destroy other members of the biologic community and not merely the single species they were intended to eradicate. The result of this action is a reduction in the biotic diversity that appears to be one of nature's important means for stabilizing the complex and dynamic entity that comprises the ecosphere. Modern agriculture, by ruthless intolerance of competitors (be they weeds or animal pests), has long acted as a great ecological simplifier, so the recent escalation into chemical control measures serves to greatly accentuate an already ecologically unsound practice. The heavy costs of artificially controlling the outbreaks of insect pests that all too frequently attack managed woodlots and extensive farmlands attest to the inevitable consequences of this ecological simplification. In the summer of 1970 spruce-budworm moths invaded Toronto and their caterpillars ravaged forests on the Ontario–Quebec border, and Bertha Army "Worms" attacked rapeseed acreage in Saskatchewan. The full impact of biocides on ecosystems is beyond the scope of this book, but is well documented elsewhere (see, for example, Rudd 1964, Woodwell 1967, Ehrlich and Ehrlich 1970: 167 *ff.*).

Unfortunately, it has been forecast that the successful control of many fungal, nematode, and insect pests of agricultural crops is not less than thirty years away in the view of at least one competent authority (Cooke 1970: 27). The more intensively the land is used for productive purposes the more likely is the increasing economic and ecologic cost of effective control. Indeed, the $64,000 question now is no longer "Can we continue to produce more food?" but rather "What are the environmental consequences of attempting to produce more food?"

THE MYTH OF THE INEXHAUSTIBLE SEA

Discussions of possible future population–food supply crises invariably move from consideration of land-based food production techniques and reforms to consideration of the presumed large stocks of marine protein that are generally held to be capable of great productive expansion. This optimistic view of the untapped potential of the seas is based on a number of underlying premises and assumptions which must be continually and carefully evaluated in light of current studies and statistical reports on the productivity of the marine environment.

For the most part, the distribution of the major fisheries of the world encompasses the most accessible regions, close inshore at points easily fished, and, furthermore, generally adjacent to the technologically more advanced nations. The optimistic implication of such a situation is that as all these coastal regions collectively comprise no more than 10 per cent of the oceans' area, then further unimpeded expansion of fishery activity in the future will take place seaward, out from the continental shelf, at a time when both technology and markets allow. It is further assumed that the concentration of commercial fisheries in the North Atlantic and North Pacific oceans results merely from the proximity to these regions of large human populations inhabiting the north temperate zone. The corollary of this belief is that when the market demand is strong enough, these and other nations will expand their fishery activity to the mid-latitudes and to the Southern Hemisphere where modern commercial fishing activity is at present relatively underdeveloped.

There is no doubt that many of these implied future activities will be attempted: we *can* expect expansion of fishing activity to new fishing grounds, both as dependency upon, and hence demand for, the product increases and as technologic advances are made in fishing vessels and gear. The crucial question, however, is often not asked: namely, at even the present rate of exploitation, just how long can such expansion continue until the stocks either are seriously overfished or decline at a rate which makes commercial fishing an uneconomic, and hence impractical, large-scale food-producing activity?

Before seeking an answer to that important question, let us

remember that the problem of overfishing is not a new one, and is not solely dependent on the ruthlessly efficient fish-locating and catching equipment now in use. Overfishing in the North Atlantic and the adjacent North Sea started eighty years ago, when plaice stocks failed to maintain their abundance in the face of sustained harvesting by several European nations. Plaice stocks in the White Sea and off the Icelandic coast were in similar decline during the inter-war years, as were the previously important sources of cod, haddock, and hake. Since the end of World War II overfishing has extended from the European fishing grounds to the northwestern North Atlantic, so that such species as ocean perch and stocks of cod off Newfoundland, Labrador, Nova Scotia, and Greenland, as well as in the Barents Sea, off Iceland and the Faeroes, have in turn suffered serious depletion.

The political difficulty in attempting to successfully rationalize these internationally important fisheries is discussed in an article by Dr. S. J. Holt, a fishery biologist with the Food and Agriculture Organization, and I will reiterate his firm conclusion that "it is quite evident that there really is no escape from the paramount need, if high yields are to be sustained: this is to *limit* the fishing effort deployed in the intensive fisheries" (Holt 1969: 192).

Therefore, any perspective on future world fishery potential must be couched in terms of sustained yields and the need to limit activities in the presently highly profitable, and mostly international, fisheries. Their production in recent years has been one of the very few major high quality food industries showing rates of growth greater than that of the human population. The hope that this statistical fact represented, as a possible solution to world hunger and nutritional problems, now appears in question; according to recent F.A.O. reports world fishery production in 1969 declined over the previous year's catch, suggesting that problems associated with grave overfishing of major fish stocks may now have become noticeably critical.

Apart from these questions of sustained production now becoming apparent, there are continuing problems associated with distribution and consumption if the protein supply of the sea is to serve as a bulwark against mass hunger and malnutrition; about 75 per cent of the 65 million metric tons of world fishery production is taken by only fourteen nations and these include most of the agriculturally advanced nations whose food supply is already more than adequate. Indeed, about half the total fishery production is converted into animal feed to maintain the high level of agricultural production of the industrialized countries, thus leading to an anomalous trade pattern whereby protein-poor countries export high-grade protein to the protein-rich countries so that these affluents can maintain their highly profitable livestock industries and privileged diets.

Another important consideration is that once a fishery begins to suffer from the effects of overfishing, the almost invariable adaptive response of economic man is to further develop his technologic efficiency in an effort to maintain economically profitable exploitation of that resource. This ecologically maladaptive behaviour has two serious consequences: it rapidly accelerates the on-going destruction of that fish stock; and, it ensures that when another virgin, or otherwise profitable, stock is located elsewhere, a very intensive and highly efficient exploitative activity is brought to bear with damaging effect often before the necessary research and ensuing safeguards can be instigated to protect the long-term viability of that stock. The rapidity of this induced decline in fishery stocks is well illustrated by considering the events reported at two United Nations fishery conferences held in 1949 and 1968. At the 1949 meeting a map was produced showing the location of thirty major commercial stocks believed at that time to be under-fished. By 1968, about half of those stocks were reported to be fished close to, or beyond, the sustainable level. The 1969 world statistics already mentioned suggest that, in the face of an enormous technologic and economic investment and effort, some crisis may well be closer at hand than most would care to admit. In 1972 the international body set up by nations fishing the North Atlantic almost broke apart during its annual meeting because of failure to resolve a number of critical issues made more acute by diminishing quantities of fish.

How realistic is it to believe that the present world fish harvest, taken from such a small percentage of the ocean's surface, can be increased by expanding the fisheries to more remote and offshore regions? Undoubtedly, as said earlier, some expansion will occur, and will depend on certain technological advances being made and also on the development of fishery products utilizing marine species not presently marketed or marketable. One of the best reviews of the subject suggests that fishery expansion at the present rate can only continue for a decade at most (Ryther 1969: 76). This prognosis is based on unalterable biological parameters of marine protein production, which indicate that 90 per cent of the ocean's surface presently provides little to the fishery catch statistics for the very good reason that it is a virtual biological desert. Therefore, not only does it contribute insignificantly today, but it has almost no potential for improvement in the future either.

Clearly, then, the remaining 10 per cent—comprising the continental shelf areas and the offshore banks along with a few restricted areas of oceanic upwelling—must bear the vast burden of future expansion together with some presently putatively under-fished areas of the Indian Ocean. It should not go unnoticed that the highly productive shelf regions (generating about 50 per cent of the world's fishery production) are also the most threatened by pollution, a danger which is even now extending offshore to the banks where oil and mineral prospecting is gaining momentum. Unfortunately, too, such valued proximate fishing grounds are exceedingly difficult to control because of the historically complex conflicting patterns of international utilization.

Let us return for a moment to the observation made above, namely that under-exploited fishing grounds are believed still to exist in some areas of the globe. It is important to stress that the technical ability exists at present to saturate any productive fishing area and in a few short years of rapacious activity to reduce or destroy its future utility for the benefit of ever more hungry mouths. For example, we might note that recently a single Rumanian fishing vessel, equipped with the most modern locational and catching gear, outfished all 1500 vessels of the New Zealand fleet operating in the South Pacific (Ehrlich 1970: 57). Fishery experts believe that without adding one more ship the fishing fleets of the world afloat today are quite adequate to double the tonnage of marine resources landed each year. Japan, now a leading nation in all the major fishing areas of the world, has fleets operating at locations north and south, to the east and west, at distances up to 8000 miles from that small densely populated island. Japan has had a fishery tradition longer than some of its challengers for supremacy, but the time cannot be too far away before the massive and still enlarging hardware of the Soviet and East European fishing fleets overtake the Japanese lead in terms of shipping tonnage and catching ability. At the moment three nations—Japan, Peru, and Russia—account for about 40 per cent of world fishery production; the United States and Norway contribute another 10 per cent. China, with more than twice the population of Japan, Peru, and Russia combined, also places a very high value on fish protein, but as yet has scarcely ventured outside her own coastal and inland waters (Borgstrom 1970).

In conclusion, it appears that if the marine environment is to provide any respite from present and future world food shortages, such relief is unlikely to result from any intensification of the existing means of using the oceans' biological potential, namely through "hunting and trapping" of wild, though sometimes managed, fish and mammal populations. As an example of new directions that must be sought, it can be noted that unfertilized fish ponds often exceed by several times the productivity of the natural marine environment, and that fertilization of these ponds has resulted in a twentyfold increment in fish yield compared with natural production (see, for example, Fye *et al.* 1968: 61–62). Some countries, such as Japan, are presently realizing an increasing proportion of their annual production of marine protein through such husbandry practices, and a vast spread of such innovative techniques is a likely event in the decades to come. Such hopeful procedures, however, are utterly dependent upon a healthy, unpolluted coastal environment, a requirement that appears more and more unrealizeable given our present penchant for using natural waterways as our industrial vascular system and the oceans as the ultimate dumping ground for our every waste product.

COSTS AND PROGNOSES

There are very many ways to view man's activities as the great despoiler, and they tend to be ranked in importance according to pertinent values we hold in the areas of morality, aesthetics, and economics, among others.

Some would maintain that extinction of biologic species and communities is an integral part of life, that well over 95 per cent of all species and associations were extinct long before *Homo sapiens* appeared 200,000 years ago, the implication clearly being that there is something very proper and inevitable about the continual demise of some forms of life. The extension of this viewpoint, however, in order to pardon man's ecologically disruptive behaviour, seems to me to shortchange man's claim to rationality and purposiveness. Are those advocates saying, in effect, that the geophysical forces that created an environment conducive to the evolution of land plants half a billion years ago, or that set in motion changes resulting in the explosive spread of mammals at the expense of giant reptiles seventy million years ago, that these forces are equivalent to such cultural events as the development of agriculture, the creation of savanna grasslands, or more recently the threat posed to the future existence of many economically and ecologically important species of birds, mammals, and fish whose survival status is still in doubt?

It is important to continually stress that man, despite his advanced technology, remains one component part of the interrelated web of ecologic systems that envelop this planet. Indeed, the very scale of man's technologic activity is now so vast, the effects on the environment now so much more complex and far-reaching, that this same technology has served to further integrate and intensify our relationship to this global ecosystemic network, rather than separate or emancipate us from its constraints.

An example of this limiting effect on man is presented by our relationship to one environmental resource: water. Water, more than any other single resource, is likely to ultimately limit our further spread over the face of the Earth; there is not one more drop of water in existence now on the Earth's surface or in its atmosphere than there was when this planet first cooled some billions of years ago. The hydrological cycle which determines the distribution and availability of water is governed by inexorable forces quite unaffected by our puny and now increasingly desperate attempts to redistribute or otherwise ensure a ready provision of clean water for our various uses. Despite an appearance of plenty, much of the global supply is not directly usable by us: 97 per cent is salty, and 98 per cent of the remainder is locked up in icecaps and glaciers. The relatively small amount of liquid fresh water is being utilized at an alarming rate, more especially in the densely populated industrial or intensively agricultural countries of Europe, where the rate of capital depletion is three times faster than the hydrological cycle can return clean fresh water to the system. In North America, water is removed from the existing sources of supply twice as fast as it can be replaced.

Current forecasts suggest that 700 billion gallons of fresh water will be required annually in North America in 1980, at current standards of consumption. Best estimates indicate that the maximum available will be 650 billion gallons (Borgstrom, quoted in Ehrlich and Ehrlich 1970: 65).

The great demand for water in North America stems not just from domestic machinery—such as flush-toilets and automatic washing machines—but from the requirements of industry, both technological and agricultural. It has been estimated (see, for example, Borgstrom 1967) that it takes 100,000 gallons of water to produce one automobile and about 2,500 gallons to produce one pound of beef-steak. Clearly, unless industry finds new ways to function, or people curb their rapacious appetites for cars, sirloin, and other water-intensive products, crisis conditions appear inevitable in the not-too-distant future.

Canada has about one-quarter of the world standing crop of fresh water, and about one-half of one per cent of the world's population; we might therefore appear to be exempt from these dismal prognoses. Is it realistic, though, to believe that our populous neighbour, the world's most powerful nation, would allow its privileged economic influence to wane and its social fabric to tear to shreds when the vital resource needed to postpone that time of reckoning lies politically and economically within its orbit—and physically within its grasp?

Obviously such hard-nosed economic reasons for prudent behaviour are important causes for husbanding our natural resources rather than subjecting them to profligate abuse. There are other reasons, perhaps ultimately even more important than the pragmatic considerations entered above.

To Dr. David Suzuki, a University of British Columbia biologist, an integral part of man's very humanity is threatened by his disregard of the environment:

> Man alone of all creatures can look at a whooping crane or a whale and know "That is beautiful," and his appreciation of that animal is an important part of man's dignity. When we destroy another species, we in fact demonstrate a contempt for ourselves because we destroy a bit of that spiritual essence that makes man unique. Our disregard for other living organisms is simply an extension of our own self-contempt, which is revealed by the exploitation, suffering and murder of human beings at the hands of other men. (Suzuki 1970: 6.)

Dr. David Ehrenfeld, a Columbia University biologist, equates destruction of any significant part of the web of life as outright, irrevocable theft, just as wanton and reprehensible as the destruction of a priceless work of art:

> All species are potential Humpty Dumpties: the processes of evolution, as we know them, will not put them together again on this planet once they are destroyed. There are numerous, valid aesthetic and practical reasons for supporting the conservation of species (and of communities), but this spectre of irreversibility is the most powerful reason of all. We are privileged to have witnessed some of the finest examples of the great adaptive radiations that took place during the Mesozoic and Cenozoic Eras. We have seen giant tortoises, giraffes, elephants, orchids, macaws, redwoods, orangutans, walruses and whales—fabulous creatures that would enliven any mythology, even if they were not real. Our immediate descendants will be unable to see living representatives of many of the species in these groups, and no one should blame future generations if they consider our personal accounts and recollections an inadequate substitute for living specimens, nor will their loss be less if they are unaware that such species existed. (Ehrenfeld 1970: 3–4.)

We rightly feel angry, when, for example, we hear that poachers are trying to kill off the remaining few dozen Javan Rhinoceros, or that extermination of the fabulous Blue Whale (the largest creature ever to have lived) is a distinct possibility because of continued exploitation by Asian or European whaling interests. Our anger, our lack of sympathy for those we accuse, stems from their holding different cultural values from ours: they believe in, and need, rhino parts for their medical and magical arts; they value whale meat in their diet, and consequently their national dietary habits and their economy make cetacean steak and oil important commodities. By this same token, is there not great risk that our current short-sighted, avaricious, and seemingly irresponsible behaviour will appear unjustifiable, reprehensible, and anger-provoking to those who do not share our particular values—including, perhaps, our descendants who will follow in a generation or two?

To consider briefly the further implication of the prayer in the final pregnant sentence quoted above from Dr. Ehrenfeld's book, namely the magnitude of the loss to future generations of species and biological communities destroyed by those generations' immediate forebears. Many have commented on the moral obligation to respect posterity, to continue responsible stewardship of our environmental heritage. I believe the most salient feature of this viewpoint has to do with what our dehumanizing and devaluing the lives of others does to us, or to paraphrase author James Baldwin: One cannot deny the humanity of another without diminishing one's own; in the face of one's victim, one sees oneself.

Economist Kenneth Boulding states this ethic even more prophetically, when attempting to answer the question "what has posterity ever done for me?" He writes:

> The only answer to this, as far as I can see, is to point out that the welfare of the individual depends on the extent to which he can identify himself with others, and that the most satisfactory individual identity is that which identifies not only with a community in space but also with a community extending over time from the past into the future . . . there is a great deal of historical evidence to suggest that a society which loses its identity with posterity and which loses its positive image of the future loses also its capacity to deal with present problems and soon falls apart. (Boulding 1966: 11.)

So, if history, reason, and commonsense have anything to tell us at this juncture, it is: take care, man, in the face of one's victim one may very well see an uncomfortable likeness.

The world food supply probably has, in the past, exerted some significant limiting effect on growth of the human population: indeed, to some extent (through malnutrition/undernourishment–aggravated deaths) it still does. Even though modern man *has* created a magnificent technology to facilitate greater production of food, this upward trend cannot continue indefinitely. Indeed, the ecologic costs of doing what is being done are certainly not insignificant, and it remains true that modern agriculture is quite impossible without the huge economic subsidies provided by an industrial-economic base. As we wish to eat in the manner we have grown accustomed to, we bear the financial costs of producing the food, but the ecosystem does not owe us a livelihood, and we would be prudent to study its condition with the same concern that industrialists pay to the stock market reports.

The abuses perpetrated for the sale of increased yields are not inconsequential: for example, the heavy use of chemical fertilizers, with consequent disruption of the nitrogen and phosphorus cycles and contamination of ground water supplies; the application of insecticides with their insidious, long-term, and mostly unknown, physiological and ecological side effects; and the not inconsiderable environmental costs of manufacturing these chemical aids without which modern agriculture would immediately collapse (see, for example, Brown 1970).

Two million years were required for man's numbers to reach the first billion; it is taking fifteen years (1960–1975) to add the fourth billion. The numbers game oversimplifies man's predicament, for not only is the number of people increasing alarmingly, but the aspirations of more and more people are matching those of the most affluent. It is the environmental costs of supporting the relatively few affluent peoples, who *do* have the means to increase their demand on the environment, that threaten the continued integrity of the biosphere. The more privileged the nation, the more easily and likely are the aspirations of its peoples to be realized, and the more the cost to all of so achieving.

Few would deny Canada's privileged place in the world today, nor her desire or ability to progress (consume); our self-respect as concerned, rational beings should demand of us that we curb our immodest national appetite by reducing sharply our collective consumptive demands. This could be achieved by several means, none of which alone will have the effective strength to succeed. We must certainly make the consequences of our technology less environmentally damaging—for example, by reclaiming and recycling products whenever possible. We must curb our unnecessary yet sensitized appetites for trivial and intrinsically valueless products and services—for instance, does a family need to take home about five pounds of paper bags and fancy wrappers from the supermarket each week? (After all, it takes about seventeen trees and 240,000 gallons of water to manufacture one ton of paper.) Finally, we must certainly take steps to reduce the rate at which we add new consumers to the ranks of the present population.

chapter four

THE POPULATION ISSUE IN CANADA

Canada entered the twentieth century with 5.4 million inhabitants; by 1950 the number had increased 250 per cent and by 1980 the 1950 population will likely have doubled in size to reach 25.4 million. Projections till the end of the century vary, but a median estimated population size appears to be 34 million.

The fact that the human population is rising at an accelerating pace all over the world should not delude us into thinking that this is wholly a "natural" happening and therefore intrinsically good or somehow inevitable. Indeed, it is a very recent phenomenon in terms of human history, and results in large measure from modern man's technologic tampering with natural controls whose existence ensured the continued environment–population balance. To be sure, technologic advances such as improved agronomy and mechanical skills have increased the carrying capacity of the habitat, but it must be obvious to everyone that such increments cannot continue indefinitely, given the finite nature of our resources.

Modern medicine is one technologic advance whose short-term consequences are undoubtedly in the very best interest, but whose longer term implications we have scarcely begun to plan for in any rational way. Indeed, such improvidence on the part of mankind, when the probable outcome is so easily inferred, must seriously challenge our right to unselfconscious generic claim to rationality. Given a physically bounded habitat, such as exists on planet Earth, there are only two ways that population increase can be halted: either through a reduction in birth-rate, or through an increase in death-rate. There is absolutely, and without any doubt whatsoever, no other way.

These two alternate adaptive strategies must be kept to the fore, not only when thinking about population matters, but when thinking in any way at all about the future, and, given present trends, even when considering the rather immediate future.

It is important to stress at this juncture, and elsewhere in this book, that the threat to Canadians of a continuing increase in national population size is not to life itself but to the *quality* of life to be experienced in the immediate future. We do have the national resources to feed, house, and educate a larger population, after a fashion, for some time to come. But it is best not to overstress this apparent good fortune, for we are inextricably linked to global ecologic, economic, and political networks whose future dysfunction would very rapidly, completely, and irrevocably destroy *our* potential for continued well-being.

On the issue of a continued improvement in the quality of national life in the face of population increase, I can do no better than quote the words of a Harvard University sociologist, who wrote:

> Each year we spend an ever larger portion of our high Gross National Product merely to escape the consequences of congestion and additions to our number. Population increase does not lead to crowded schools in a country of low education levels, to traffic jams if only a few own cars, to overcrowded vacation spots, if only a few have vacations, to losses of land for roads and municipal facilities if only a few live in suburbs. But in combination with

our high material levels of living population increase in this country has already necessitated greater restrictions on individual behavior, greater centralization in government, rising economic costs and taxes, crowded schools and recreation areas, vanishing countryside, air and water pollution, endless traffic jams, crowded court schedules, and a steady loss in time, solitude, quiet, beauty and peace of mind. (Day 1967: 56–57.)

The fact that these comments were written specifically about the situation in the United States is immaterial, for the description given is only too familiar to most urban North Americans today (see, for example, editorial comment in the Hamilton *Spectator,* 22 July 1972). The unwholesome situation described overtakes a larger proportion of Canadians each year, for the demands on our space, air, water, and other valued resources and amenities are increased by continental pressures of rising population numbers and appetites. So within the lifetime of most readers of this book there will be not only twice as many Canadians travelling the roads looking for a vacation spot or unpolluted lake to swim in but twice as many continental North Americans, too, perhaps 450 million of us sharing what is left. In view of the pertinence of this continental approach to any ecologic understanding of Canadian environmental issues, to restrict one's viewpoint to merely national trends and occurrences tends to unreal parochialism which can only result in a partial understanding of the complexities of the total situation. Yet, to many, Canadian problems seem small enough to be manageable—in comparison, for example, with those now extant in the United States—with a result that hopelessness and defensive retreat are a likely result of confrontation with the continental dimensions of the difficulties that have to be faced. As later parts of this book will hopefully demonstrate, morever, many of our major environmental problems are indeed created right here in Canada and must be overcome on home ground. The only way to view the continental, and indeed the global, issues involving us, is surely to contribute positively toward their solution by rational behaviour both at home and, if possible, abroad. Many environmentalists are increasingly pessimistic about the outcome of the rapidly approaching population–

environment crisis, but we will certainly increase our chances immeasurably if *we* act rationally and at the same time apply whatever influence we can muster to exhort others to do the same.

Given our smaller-sized problems, compared with those of the populous developed and less developed nations of the world, our greater chances of success may render the size of our international contribution important out of all proportion to our numerical insignificance on the international scene. For these vital national and international reasons the issues surrounding a national population policy must be urgently and thoroughly debated by Canadians with understanding, tolerance, imagination, and resolve.

SOME DEMOGRAPHIC CONSIDERATIONS

It is very easy to be misled by the intricacy and semantics of demographic analysis into believing that the current Canadian decline in crude birth-rate signals an end to the possibility of overpopulation and in its place a need to concern ourselves with the danger of national extinction. It must be stressed that the measure "crude birth-rate" is not only a very rough reflection of human fertility but as a statistic provides almost no basis for prediction of future population size. Without going into details, it can be stated that a declining crude birth-rate can, and often does, coexist with a fairly rapid increase in population size. Crude birth-rate is the ratio obtained when the total number of live births in any year is divided by the total number of people alive at the mid-point of that same year. It is evident that this ratio will vary according to alterations in either the numerator or the denominator, and that changes in either will reflect demographic events quite unrelated to actual reproductive performance: for example, the proportion of women in the population in any year who are physiologically capable of conceiving, or who are married, or become widowed or divorced.

We are now, in Canada, seeing the entry into marriage and motherhood of the young women who were born during the post-war "baby-boom." That period of high fertility was related to, among other factors, the expanding economic activity of the times; thus the period of the "baby-boom" extended many years after the termination of World War hostilities, in fact, from about 1946 to 1959. The number of babies born during this period climbed steadily from just below 289,000 in 1945 to more than 464,000 in 1959.

Children born in the 1950s are for the most part only now entering their reproductive life. There are two important demographic consequences of this earlier baby-boom. Firstly, given that most urban families have either two or three children, even a progressive statistical decrease in desired family size can be more than offset by the increasing recruitment of young women into the ranks of motherhood. Secondly, because of the relationship existing between generation time, number of offspring produced, and age at which mothers produce children (given the current trend to earlier marriage and an expanding population), even with fewer children per marriage the rate of population growth so compounded will still be very large. The mathematics of the relationship are explained in texts on population dynamics (for example, MacArthur and Connell 1966: 130), and need not detain us further here. To illustrate this relationship, however, a woman who has her first baby at age 18 and has one more each year till age 22, contributes in equal fashion to the rate of population growth as another woman who has twice as many children but has her first child at age 30.

The dynamic relationships translate into awesome human equations: given the current vital statistics of the United States, for example, if the average U.S. family were increased from two to three children, the difference would be a shift from a stable population of around 200 million maintained well into the twenty-first century to a progressively expanding population which would reach 400 million about forty years from now.

In Canada today the average completed family size is about 3.25 children, but according to some measures it appears to be declining slightly; still, this country has one of the highest rates of population growth of any developed nation in the world: 1.7 per cent increase per year, compared with 1.0 per cent in the United States, 1.0 per cent in the Soviet Union, and 0.8 per cent in Europe. In fact, Canada's growth rate is nearer that of some less developed regions of the Third World: Middle Africa 2.2 per cent, South-West Asia 2.4 per cent, South-East Asia 2.2 per cent, temperate South America 1.8 per cent. As in the less developed countries, then, we are moving rapidly away from a situation of population stability, and with a continuation of our current high rate of increase the Canadian population would double in about forty-one years. A recent study by two University of Montreal demographers suggests that the sharp statistical decline in fertility among married Canadian women since 1959 has occurred mostly through their postponement of childbearing (Légaré and Henripin 1971: 116). The inevitable conclusion must follow that no significant reduction in population growth will occur unless this postponement either extends till near the end of the reproductive phase of these women's lives or indeed becomes transformed into fewer children.

Any purely voluntary changes in reproductive behaviour that slow down the present continuing growth of population will initially require a modification in people's perception of a smaller family size as being desirable, and then concurrently a matching alteration in behaviour so as to realize effectively the goal of this smaller family size. Such changes evidently have strong social, cultural, and psychological components and will be discussed further in Chapter 5.

THE COSTS OF POPULATION GROWTH

Just how necessary is continued population growth for national prosperity, and, by extension, what would be the economic consequences of a reduction in our present 1.7 per cent per annum rate of population growth?

I pose this last question because most of us are not economists, and consequently we tend to adhere to certain simplistic and erroneous beliefs that have become entrenched in our North American culture, derived in part from our colonial heritage. The grossest of these quasi-economic propositions relates the need for an ever-expanding population if we are to enjoy continuing economic growth and prosperity. It is true that great expansion of markets and industrial production occurred during the second half of the nineteenth century and the early part of this century. The financial rewards stemming from this expanding industrial output, however, resulted from technological breakthroughs in methods of production; though vast new markets were, historically, a very necessary condition for the growth of the industrialization complex they in no way caused this increase. It would be well to remember the recent near-miraculous economic development in countries such as Japan, West Germany, France, and Italy, where population growth rates have been among the lowest in those regions of the globe.

In fact it can be argued that, given the very high private and national expenditures involved for each addition to the population, the net economic return from population increase for highly industrialized nations is decidedly negative (see, for example, Westoff and Westoff 1968: 342–43).

Whatever the supposed benefits stemming from a larger number of people, we must not lose sight of the fact that there are very tangible costs to be weighed against the benefits. The cost of population increase is, quite simply, that which must be foregone to bring that increment into existence: even if the pie is getting larger, there are more individuals wishing to obtain a slice. If it is true that more babies mean larger sales of washing machines, clothing, toys, food, and so on, it is equally true that people's forced investment in these commodities prevents their shopping for alternate growth-promoting purchases. Indeed, there are many sectors of the domestic economy, for example, travel, recreation, and entertainment, and a host of other so-called "luxury" trades, which could undergo enormous expansion under conditions of zero population growth or even declining numbers once the population in question was unburdened of the financial responsibility of investing in additional children. Indeed, we need to reflect seriously on the implications of *not* diverting more of our economic resources away from these capital- and pollution-intensive industries as our per capita disposable income more than doubles by the year 2000.

To return to the increase in population, however, the full cost of each additional birth obviously is not apparent or even accurately calculable at the time of that birth, but rather flows as a stream of costs over the next fifteen or twenty-five years, depending on when the individual enters the productive phase of life. Therefore, on a purely demographic level, a nation with a 2 per cent population growth rate has only 85 per cent the number of potentially productive workers compared with a similar sized nation of more nearly stationary population or about 0.5 per cent per annum rate of population growth (as do West Germany, the United Kingdom, Belgium, or Czechoslovakia, for example). Accordingly, not only is the productive potential only 85 per cent as large, all other things being equal, but, constituting a far greater negative impact, there is an additional 15 per cent of the population non-productive yet consuming and whose cost requirements have to be met by the smaller number of producers.

Further, we should certainly remember that the costs to be met by additions to the population are in direct proportion, not only to the size of the increment but also to the standard of living enjoyed by the members of that populace. It follows that a wealthy nation must be *very* wealthy indeed to be able to afford a high rate of population growth *and* a just level of social and economic well-being and opportunity. There are few developed and wealthy nations still recklessly burning the candle at both ends through blatant disregard for this fact of economic life, but one such nation is Canada. Canada, unlike most other aspiring countries with high rates of population increase, is wealthy enough at present to ensure that most of us will live long enough to regret this recklessness.

Dr. Joseph Spengler, the distinguished U.S. economist having particular interest in population matters, has succinctly warned: "It is not adequately recognized, however, that today's actions respecting issues with long time dimensions . . . can entrap man's future, imprison him in a set of costs not of his own making, and force him to use inputs to escape this trap instead of improve his conditions of life. In present day parlance, today's careless, future-disregarding action shrinks tomorrow's range of options. Today's excessive fertility is a case in point" (Spengler 1967: 33).

AN OPTIMUM POPULATION FOR CANADA?

There are four ways at least in which the concept of optimum can be brought to bear on the population issue. These ways relate to the more important parameters of a given population, namely, its size, composition, rate of growth, and spatial distribution.

There is no such thing as a fixed optimum for any given land area. The size and density of a population in a region depends, in this day and age, not so much on the productivity of the land as on the available technology and form of social, political, and economic organization utilized by the residents. There will be upper and lower limits of population size, and environmental considerations, often intimately linked with economic ones, can have overriding importance. To seek an optimum *size* of population is in fact almost as irrelevant as impossible, for, as Nobel-laureate economist Gunnar Myrdal has suggested, the curve that relates population size to some economic function is likely to resemble a loaf of bread, indicating that a large plateau of population size probably has no marked effect on economic performance whereas the large or small extremes do have very marked effects.

Optima expressed then as values falling between more or less decisively defined limits probably can be derived, but only in relation to certain stated goals. Thus a regional optimum size and density would vary according to whether small-scale agricultural or large-scale industrial production was the goal to be maximized, or whether the standard of living was to be that of Calgary or Calcutta. The size, density, composition, and growth-rate optima are related; for example, if, because of a change in social organization or economic adaptation, the optimal population of an area were to suddenly become definitely more or less than optimal, it follows that the previous optimum rate of growth of that population would have to be altered if the goal of optimum population size were to be re-established.

Even if population could be maintained at a fixed level, however, there is considerable internal dynamic change due to the fact that decisions taken twenty years ago (for example, whether to have a child) are now having their incremental effect on growth (if that then-child in turn is now contemplating starting a family). In addition, the social or economic conditions that twenty years ago encouraged large families may today be quite different, so that there may be a shift in the size of family considered desirable under existing conditions. The need for such changing goals has been seen most recently in Eastern

Europe and in Japan. In Japan, for example, population growth rate was slowed during the 1950s to facilitate economic reorganization and growth; the inordinate success of this measure resulted in enormous labour-intensive industrial advances that created an anticipated demand for labour which the current level of fertility would be unable to supply in a few years. Thus, a return to higher levels of fertility may now be not only acceptable but even necessary to maximize economic goals.

This short discussion into aspects of population optima should serve to make two conclusions very evident. Firstly, that any definition of "optimum" must clearly state what are the various goals that the population seeks to maximize, and, secondly, that a high degree of planning is involved both to set the goals and to decide how they are to be reached. If we remember that population dynamics includes the important lag effect (length of time elapsing from birth to adult potential), then the national planning effort must indeed be comprehensive for there is no point in having second thoughts about the worthiness of a particular goal fifteen or so years after setting in motion various actions designed primarily with that twenty-year goal in mind. If the establishment of such long-term goals seems utter fantasy to a reader only too aware of the short-term political goals chased by politicians with a five-year provisional mandate to govern, that is only so because the general voting public is not yet aware of the advisability of urgent action in this field, an urgency that demands that the management of the national population be removed from political control, a position which will be promoted later in this book. Accepting that traditional attitudes have considerable built-in resistance to change makes it all the more imperative that the prevailing *laissez-faire* attitude of Canadians toward a national population policy change in favour of more positive attitudes. Collectively we must come to realize without delay that even if our current population size appears to pose no immediate threat to us, given our lifestyle and aspirations, our rate of population growth certainly does present an instant menace. Owing to the sleeper effect of population growth, inaction now represents very seriously compounded problems in the near future; a population in the tens of millions, with high fertility and low mortality, grows at an alarming rate in a short space of time. A recent book on population problems in the United States was entitled *The 99th Hour*—for the following very good reason:

> Some people argue that we have ample room for many more people and that our agricultural system can adequately feed them without strain. Let us look at an analogy. Assume that there are two germs in the bottom of a bucket, and that they double every hour. . . . If it takes one-hundred hours for the bucket to be full of germs, at what point is the bucket one-half full of germs? A moment's thought will show that after ninety-nine hours the bucket is only half full. The title of this volume is not intended to imply that the country is half full of people, but to emphasize that it is possible to have "plenty of space left" and still be precariously near the upper limit. (Price 1967: 3–4.)

Canada's population does not double in one hour of course, but even if we assume Canada could comfortably quadruple the number of people living here, that would be only eighty years away and within the lifetime of some already here as well as our children and grandchildren not yet born. There surely cannot be any serious-minded person of goodwill alive today who believes we still have time to procrastinate on the necessity of initiating very vigorous planning action *now*.

I readily admit that analogy can be misleading and dangerous, but I contend that the demographic example offered by Price is both helpful and entirely pertinent to human population issues. Analogy between demography and the physical sciences, however, could be less than useful, especially if suggesting that optimum conditions could be predicted and engineered with anything approaching the precision and invariability expected in the physical sciences. Social scientists will be the first to admit that people and the social systems those people constitute are frustratingly unpredictable in their behaviour, and projections of future population size made by demographers in the past, using the best data and analytic methods available at that time, consistently lack the accuracy that one wishes could be obtained.

Population optima can be derived only after a series of rather general but unequivocably beneficial, national goals have been decided upon. It will follow that alteration of the constituent parts of the national equation, namely population, non-human national resources, and time, can bring the chosen goals nearer to realization, or cause them to become practically unreachable. Anything more than very general goals will be all but impossible to decide in a multi-political confederation of provinces, such as constitutes the Canadian nation. Examples of such general goals offered in the book *The Optimum Population for Britain* (Taylor 1970) are:

1. To maximize the vigour and potential of individuals;
2. To maximize the currently acceptable pattern of social organization;
3. To maximize the realization of cultural goals which enhance moral, political, and aesthetic standards;
4. To maximize real output per head;
5. To minimize pollution;
6. To minimize nutritional stress;
7. To minimize social stress.

These seven goals, under attained optimal conditions, should be conducive to indefinite maintenance (Taylor 1970: xxi).

In a similar vein, a series of ten proposals were offered to readers of *Saturday Review* in August 1968 as being socially "good" and therefore desirable values to be held and maximized by modern society; few would disagree that:

1. People are better alive than dead;
2. People are better healthy than sick;
3. People are better off literate than illiterate;
4. People are better off adequately housed than inadequately housed;
5. People are better off in beautiful than in ugly cities and towns;
6. People are better off if they have opportunity for enjoyment—music, literature, drama, and the arts;
7. Education above the elementary level should be as nearly universal as possible through secondary schools, and higher education as widely diffused as practicable;
8. Development of science and the arts should continue or possibly be expanded;

9. Minimum resources for living should be available to all;
10. Leisure and access to green country should be a human experience available to everyone. (Berle 1968: 12.)

Although I think these and similarly desirable goals would fairly easily be agreed upon (for who could deny their inherent goodness, even if decrying their usefulness or possibility of attainment?), there is no doubt that the means or avenues to attain them would likely be cause for considerable disagreement. At this stage, however, I believe we would be making a very real start on the road to rational realization of these desirable objectives if the majority of Canadians were to explicitly acknowledge that demographic considerations are pertinent to such national goals and, more explicitly, that population size and growth rate relate to social and economic advancement in ways which are not always positive.

ZERO POPULATION GROWTH

An eventual halt to the progressive increase in numbers of people is, of course, inevitable, for no population can go on expanding indefinitely into the future. Thus to advocate adoption of the goal of a zero rate of population growth is a safe enough cause to espouse; dissent will be generated, however, when discussion centres on the question of how, or when, the goal is to be attained (see, for example, Notestein 1970, and comments following by demographers Hauser, Blake, and Demeny). Two extreme courses exist: either allow nature to effect population stabilization (as Malthus warns), or seek and apply man-made, rational solutions.

In 1968 an organization known as Zero Population Growth (ZPG) was formed in the United States with the objective of taking political action if necessary on important population and environmental issues. Dr. Paul R. Ehrlich of Stanford University, one of the spiritual leaders of this movement, wrote in 1970: "It may well be necessary for a new political party to be formed, one founded on the principles of population control, environmental quality and a stabilized economy . . . it could, indeed, grow out of Zero Population Growth" (Ehrlich and Ehrlich 1970: 291).

On 11 August 1971, Associated Press carried the news that the Coalition for a National Population Policy had been set up in the United States by former U.S. Senator Joseph D. Tydings and University President Milton Eisenhower of Johns Hopkins University. The objectives of this group will be to work actively toward the national goal of a zero rate of population growth, or, stated another way, an eventually stable U.S. population.

ZPG groups have appeared in many North American cities and in other countries too. A ZPG group exists in Toronto and a national meeting was held in that city, in June 1971, to discuss the feasibility of establishing a national political force equivalent to the U.S. Coalition for a National Population Policy.

In view of the widespread appeal and impetus of the ZPG ideal, could it usefully become the basis for a population policy? Basically, a zero rate of population growth implies that a stationary population is maintained indefinitely because a balanced recruitment into the population (through inmigration and births) equals losses from that population (through outmigration and deaths). A zero rate of population growth is the effective equivalent (ignoring the effects of migration) of a net reproductive rate of 1.0, in a stable population, where net reproductive rate (NRR) is a measure of the increase in a stable population that occurs over a time period, *normally equivalent to the average interval between generations,* under existing mortality and fertility rates. I have deliberately introduced the demographic equivalent of a zero rate of population growth and explicitly stressed (through italics) that we are dealing with a *rate* rather than an absolute. A rate implies not only that the phenomenon is measured over a time interval (in this instance a generation length of nearly thirty years), but also that normally time must elapse before the result of that event has measurable effect.

Therefore, even if a zero rate of population growth were adopted immediately a no-growth situation would not occur, *unless* a NRR of less than 1.0 were to exist; in the Canadian context this would restrict the average married couple to having one child rather than two, or, alternatively, a large proportion of the adult population to remaining childless. Clearly then, the goal of immediate attainment of a stable population will invoke high social and psychological costs for most of the Canadian population, who appear to be attitudinally and behaviourally at some distance from the required low fertility condition. Recognizing that the attainment of this goal will incur restrictions, ZPG advocates nevertheless maintain that a moral basis for their ideal exists because the objective, namely, to safeguard posterity, is good, and because the costs of survival would be borne by those alive today who threaten destruction of the system, rather than by innocent future generations as yet unborn.

If we did manage to instigate a less extreme national policy and allow each married couple an average of a little over two children—that is, if we instantly attain a NRR of 1.0—we can confidently expect our population to continue growing at least until the year 2045 when it will have reached about 27 million.

The explanation for this continued population increase with the attainment of a NRR of 1.0 lies in the unalterable fact that our immediately preceding history of high fertility above the replacement level ensures that for the next thirty years or so we will reap the reproductive harvest of the growing numbers of young people *already born* who will be starting their own families. Should this rising generation decide to adopt fertility levels even considerably below those of their parents or of the current generation of young parents, the outcome will still be a steadily increasing population size. This steady gain results not only from the fact that we have a large young population now entering the reproductive ranks, but also from the concomitant fact that we have a correspondingly small proportion in the older age groups being lost from the population. Thus Canada has proportionately 32 per cent more young people under 15 years of age and 50 per cent fewer old people over 65 years than for example the slower growing populations of European countries such as Britain or West Germany.

Calculations based on the U.S. population indicate that no matter how fast the reproductive rate declines to replacement rate, or a NRR of 1.0, for many years to come continued growth of that country's population is assured. For example, assuming a NRR of 1.0 were miraculously achieved almost at once, an increase of 40 per cent would occur before the population stabilized. As immediate attainment of that degree of reproductive restraint is clearly impossible, but assuming it could, through great efforts, be reached after a decade, then the result would be a 50 per cent increase in population before stabilization in about seventy years' time (Frejka 1968).

In short, even though a zero rate of population growth cannot be attained rapidly, or before inevitable increase in population has taken place, nevertheless it is true that the longer the delay in adopting the goals of ZPG, the larger the ultimate population will become. If a zero rate of population growth represents an ecologically sound policy, as increasing numbers of concerned and knowledgeable persons strenuously advise, then just how compromised are we now in our efforts to attain this goal, because of our past and present moderately high levels of fertility?

As mentioned earlier, Canada can boast the highest rate of population fertility of any advanced nation in the world; our peculiar position, poised demographically between the developed and less-developed nations, is expressed not only by our 1.7 per cent per annum rate of population growth but also by our youthful population profile. Reference to the national vital statistics of the developed and developing (but less-progressive) nations indicates that, expressed in terms of per cent of population below the age of 15 years, Canada (34 per cent) numerically tops the short list of developed and incipiently developed countries that bridge the gulf between the advanced European nations (21–25 per cent) and the evolving nations of Latin America, Africa, and Asia (40–47 per cent). Clearly we cannot escape the future consequences of this large proportion of young people already born; do we know anything of *their* probable reproductive performance?

There is a downward trend in family size, amounting to about 0.2 children per family per decade; however, with a present average completed family size of 3.25 children, it will clearly be some time after the year 2000 before Canada reaches a NRR of 1.0 if we only see a continuation of the current secular trend acting to depress our population fertility. Some events that might accelerate the rate of fertility decline will be mentioned in Chapters 5 and 6.

At the national level the viability of the ZPG ideal appears to hinge to a great extent on whether present-day North Americans can, in the absence of a painfully evident crisis, agree voluntarily to take steps whose adoption would obviate the need to ever be subjected to more coercive measures. The case for voluntary restraint does not seem, at this time, to be strong: a recent study conducted among members of ZPG has indicated that despite their public commitment to an ideal which would require most Americans to have only one-child families, these same individuals nevertheless intended to have two natural children (L. D. Barnett 1971).

There are two main demographic variables that have to be considered initially, when advocating a managed population; these are the maximum-sized population utlimately to be allowed and the speed with which the goal of a given sized nongrowing population is to be attained.

Without conjecturing on these two values here, but germane to the eventual discussion of those objectives, I intend to question one main assumption of the ZPG advocates, namely that *rapid* attainment of a stationary population is a desirable demographic goal (other aspects of the no-growth situation are discussed in Ayres and Kneese 1971). The basis for questioning the wisdom of rapidly achieving a zero rate of population growth is that it would produce a population unlike any hitherto known to our society, one with properties having unintended and unwanted social consequences.

As the proportion of people in the 20–40 age group produce fewer children than the number required to replace themselves, so this small cohort of children moving into reproductive age groups will in turn produce fewer offspring than the number required to replace themselves. The result will be an aging population, which within two generations will have more people over 60 years of age than under 15. A society with the demographic characteristics of a retirement resort will be most unlikely to provide the sort of progressive environment the members of ZPG so ardently desire, and incidently one most unlikely to deal successfully with the manifold adjustment problems that will be required to restructure society according to the new pattern demanded by an over-abundance of oldsters.

A growing population always has more individuals in younger age classes, so that a tapering, pyramid-shaped population profile obtains. A stationary population will have an age-distribution "pyramid" with vertical sides up to about the 50-

year class, so that a rocket-shaped, rather than pyramid-shaped, profile occurs. The pyramid-shaped distribution of ages in a population is adaptive, however, because a society has fewer high-status, high-reward positions relative to lower-status positions, and requires allocation of the scarce social and economic rewards in a manner offering at least hope of advance to new recruits entering the work force. Younger people entering the work force of a stable population soon become aware of a preponderance of older, more experienced workers just ahead of them; they work therefore in the full knowledge that their chances of advancement remain small, a realization also shared by those above them who naturally aspire to advancing still further. It seems reasonable to infer that the greatly reduced expectation of a rational rate of social and economic advance will, because of its effect upon incentive and ambition, represent a heavy individual cost and, one suspects, depict an unintended and often underevaluated consequence of of a no-growth demographic policy.

I will be the first to agree that continued high rates of population growth are luxuries few individual countries and the global ecosystem can afford any longer, and also that a zero rate of population growth is an inevitable eventuality. The social consequences outlined above have been made explicit for two main reasons: (1) I am inclined to believe that when a stable population does become established, there is likely to be little need for restrictive population policies, for, under social conditions that will likely prevail, people will scarcely be favourably disposed to produce larger numbers of children having such limiting individual prospects; and (2) Accepting that society will eventually have to adapt to the social consequences of a stable, aged, population, a more gradual rather than a more sudden transition to a zero rate of population growth appears a more prudent course of action to advocate.

NASCENT AWARENESS AND REACTIONARY POLITICS

Just how aware are Canadians that their country may indeed have a population problem? It appears that at present Canadians at almost every level of society lack any degree of consensus on this issue. For the most part this diversity of opinion is to be expected, given, on the one hand, the low degree of international concern with over-population, and on the other hand readily apparent lack of interest by the Canadian government in the world-wide, as well as domestic, ramifications of these warning pronouncements by the "experts." Indeed, in Canada, those implicit population-related policies and programs that do exist mostly aim to increase, rather than curb, the number of Canadians, whether it be through immigration, or through such pronatalistic legislation as "baby-bonuses," tax concessions for dependent children, difficulty in obtaining sterilization and abortion, and (until recently) legal restraints on advertising or promoting the use of contraceptives.

Now, however, increasing public expression—by politicians, by the news media, and by various groups of concerned citizens—suggests a growing awareness that indeed it would be prudent to rationalize, or at least discuss, the hitherto unquestioned benefits assumed to result from progressive increase in numbers of Canadians. Doubtless the efforts of pollution-fighters and environmentalists throughout North America have contributed in some measure to the recent serious questioning of the supposed benefits of an unbridled growth ethic, including the part played by population growth in this nexus of events. As an example of the explicit role played by environmentalists, Dr. Andrew H. Macpherson, a ranking federal government biologist, presented a thought-provoking paper entitled "An Optimum Population for Canada?" at a Senior Staff Seminar of the Canadian Wildlife Service in January 1970. Dr. Donald A. Chant, the dean of Canadian eco-activists, argued in *Maclean's Magazine* in August 1970 that "big as it is, Canada doesn't need more people."

Among politicians, of course, the matter has been treated with extreme diplomatic double-talk. Thus the then federal Minister of Energy, Mines, and Resources did admit on a CFTO–TV interview (12 May 1970) that overpopulation constitutes a threat to Canadian lifestyle and environment, but the Vatican itself would probably not feel compromised in conceding the existence of so indefinite a relationship.

More recently, however, some definite statements have been made by our leaders in Ottawa. The Prime Minister in particular has been at some pains to challenge Canadian thinking on the continued uncritical acceptance of Gross National Product as the most efficacious measure of national development, and, as mentioned in Chapter 2, during a speech in Vancouver in 1971 he drew explicit attention to the resource-depleting costs of population growth.

Many Canadian newspapers have been in the van of environmental advocacy; a telling illustration was provided by the St. John's, Newfoundland, *Evening Telegram* (19 March 1971) which reminded readers that whereas in 1800 there were more than 100 acres of land for every person in the United States, the acreage had been reduced to half that figure by 1870, and by fully 90 per cent in 1970, that is, about 10 acres of land per capita, including deserts, swamps, mountains, and other uninhabitable parts of the nation. The editorial did not say, but might have, that 5 acres of land per minute are being covered by asphalt and concrete in the United States, and, to compound the problem further, another five Americans are born every minute, so that by the year 2000 the present 10–acre allotment will be reduced to 2 acres. In Canada we have a rate of population growth about 50 per cent greater than the United States but, far more dangerous, only a fraction of the national awareness of what that particular statistic portends.

On 1 March 1971 the Canadian Broadcasting Corporation announced the result of a national opinion poll on population: nearly half (49 per cent) the Canadians interviewed said world population is about the right size; slightly fewer (45 per cent) said it was too large; one-third of the sample said a decrease in population would be desirable. When asked about Canada's size, however, more than one-third (39 per cent) said this country's population was too small, and 54 per cent said it was about right. Fully one-third the sample believed Canada should actively seek to increase its population size, though more, in fact one-half the sample, disagreed.

A significant opinion registered in this C.B.C. poll was that Canadians generally saw population as a problem facing poor countries rather than rich countries. I contend that this is one area of belief that is, week by week, being replaced by an increasing awareness that population growth as a problem is international in scope and shortly will involuntarily and progressively involve the prime attention of all nations, if indeed it has not already begun to do so. It is unfortunately true that in certain of the less-developed regions of Canada the concept of under-population is circulated by politicians as a convenient alibi against their failure to stimulate self-sustaining economic development. Such assertions are patently invalid, but their continued expression helps, seemingly authoritatively, to keep alive the persistent (even if minority) viewpoint that Canada might indeed, at this time, have need of a larger population.

The distance in national awareness to be travelled can be gauged from the total disregard still persisting in certain influential, non-political, circles toward instituting or encouraging any activity which might appear to be effective in reducing fertility. Take as an example Nova Scotia, a province with development and social problems common to other less-developed regions of North America and the world. In 1970 the number of births was up from the previous year's total; the number of illegitimate births is increasing yearly too, because in 1970, for example, they accounted for 12 per cent of the total, the highest ever recorded in Nova Scotia. Not only is the number of abortions performed in the province's hospitals rising to the point of presenting practical difficulties, but, more alarming still, the number of repeaters is also climbing. All this suggests a great need for increasing awareness and facilities in respect to fertility control measures presently allowed under Canadian law. At a Federal-Provincial Conference on Family Planning held in March 1971, the Director of Child and Maternal Health in the Province of Nova Scotia reported on his province's moves to establish family-planning services. He observed: "It has not been an easy course. . . . We have had many objections from different sources and you may be surprised to hear that even two of the health unit directors, of which we have eight, wrote letters to the Deputy Minister, letters containing more pages than words the policy itself contained, begging him not to implement this policy."

The policy referred to is a rather innocuous set of proposals, lacking any guarantees of corresponding financial commitment to implement them, with the following objectives:

1. To inform Canadians about the purposes and methods of

family planning so that the exercise of free individual choice will be based on adequate knowledge;

2. To promote the training of health and welfare professional and other staff involved in family planning services;
3. To promote relevant research in family planning, including population studies and research in human behaviour and reproductive physiology;
4. To support public or private family planning programs through federal grants-in-aid and joint federal-provincial shared-cost programs.

One would think that health directors, far from opposing the measures proposed by Ottawa, would heartily applaud this enlightened view, taken finally as a result of the federal government's concern that Canada was having great difficulty in lowering the relatively high rate of infant mortality, and was being outranked with respect to that statistic by countries that did have national family-planning programs. The rationale for a province-wide study of pregnancy conditions and outcome in Nova Scotia (reported in the *Canadian Journal of Public Health,* September/October 1971) contends that upwards of 20 per cent of mentally defective children born each year in the province suffer their condition as a consequence of a variety of obstetrical hazards, which result from, for example, poor maternal health, high parity, and too short an interval between pregnancies. In addition to the direct medical consequences of inadvisable conception there are other unfortunate sequelae. The federal Minister of Health and Welfare, when announcing the federal support of family-planning programs, stated: "There is good reason to believe that effective programs for family planning would reduce the incidence of unwanted children, of child neglect, abandonment, desertion, welfare dependency and child abuse." At the same time, he stressed that the program was offered on a voluntary basis to individuals desiring that kind of assistance, without any suggestion of coercion toward any person.

It is pertinent to emphasize at this juncture that family-planning programs are not population-control programs, but work at the individual level as an adjunct to rational family formation and maintenance. At the national executive level there is still no pronouncement or even whisper of a conscious realization that population is an area for national policy formulation. Nevertheless, the unemployment situation, the crisis in housing, persistent regional disparity, and escalating health care costs, for example, should make it amply apparent that in Canada, as in the United States: "The tension between population and the economy, population and environment, population and government services, is with us at all times in different forms and degrees. . . . We cannot afford to ignore it."

Such sentiments, contained in the *Interim Report of the National Commission on Population Growth and the American Future,* are not the exclusive view of the highly complex, overdeveloped, and heavily populated United States. Countries large and small, developed and developing, are realizing that they too, "cannot afford to ignore it." Witness an official policy statement from Ghana, population about 9 million, per capita income one-fifteenth part that of the United States: "The size of our present population does not pose immediate problems for us. However, the rate at which the population is increasing will very certainly create serious social, economic and political difficulties before the end of the century. If we want to alter the rate of growth, even marginally, in two decades time, we must initiate action now." And for those among our political leaders who dream dreams for Canada or Quebec or Newfoundland by way of a bountiful birth-rate, hark again to the advice of the Ghanaian policy statement on "Population Planning for National Progress and Prosperity": "Huge populations alone do not make nations great. We are moving into an age in which quality rather than quantity determines the power of nations and their influence in international affairs. By choosing to emphasize quality in its policies on population, the Government has taken a decision which will have a major impact on the lives of future generations."

PROFESSIONAL CONCERN

One barometer of awareness and concern of an incipient population crisis in Canada might be the stand taken by those professional groups whose areas of expertise in some way impinge on the issue.

Despite the stature of those few scientific bodies who have indeed voiced concern, the total number is significantly small. Some, for example the Canadian Society of Zoologists, have concentrated their pronouncements on environmental, rather than population issues, and consideration of such groups will be omitted at this time.

Any collective show of concern by the social science community has yet to materialize, paralleling the situation some years ago in the United States and Britain, for example; among all scientists, biologists in particular first voiced urgent and telling concern over the unfettered increase in human numbers and appetites.

In Canada the resolute few began to be heard publicly in the 70s. Thus, for example, the Entomological Society of Canada (E.S.C.) in August 1970 passed the following resolution by a large majority: "That the E.S.C. through its President, actively support and encourage the development of a national policy for the limitation of Canada's human population and the stabilization of that population at an ecologically acceptable level, namely at a level at which a reasonable standard of living can be sustained for future generations with the resources available." The reasons the E.S.C. adopted this public stand were based on three major considerations:

1. The finite nature of world resources, and the present lack of acceptable technological solutions to the problems shortly to be experienced when these vital resources are irrevocably expended.

Corollary: The solution to this inevitable problem is seen to depend upon the implementation of population control and rational resource management policies to be affected with as little delay as possible. As this is indeed a global problem, it appears likely that the future advice and assistance of the technically advanced nations will more readily be heeded if those countries have adopted policies they insistently advocate for others.

2. At the time this resolution was adopted by the E.S.C. there was no Canadian government department with responsibility for population control.

Corollary: It therefore seemed unlikely that any meaningful attention would be paid to the topic, certainly not commensurate with its national urgency or importance. Furthermore, because of the essentially ecologic nature of the man–environment equation and the considerable ecological competence represented by the membership of the E.S.C., the Society has now, responsibly and publicly, stated its position as an indication of its deep concern over an issue seen as fundamental to all other human activities.

3. Owing to the urgency of this problem and the recently expressed concern of a number of senior American and Canadian scientists on the need for widespread population limitation policies, the E.S.C. believes it both urgent and timely to register overt and unambiguous support of these scientists' views at this time.

Also in 1970, the Canadian Society of Wildlife and Fishery Biologists (C.S.W.F.B.) constituted a subcommittee on Population and the Quality of Life. At the 1971 Annual Meeting of that Society the Committee tabled a resolution (subsequently adopted) which included as part of the preamble, that:

> *whereas* the world human population today is . . . increasing at an exponential rate which now adds 1.3 million new people each week to the world population . . . [and]
> *whereas* incomplete figures indicate that between one and two billion people are today undernourished, and between 4 and 10 million will starve to death this year, and there is no possibility that agricultural production can be increased rapidly enough even to maintain present standards of nutrition if the population continues to increase at the present rate . . . [and]
> *whereas* increased crowding and deprivation of large segments of the human population may be the most important factors leading to increased social and behavioral disruptions . . . [and]
> *whereas* all the preceding facts indicate that a massive population decline is inevitable . . . [and]
> *whereas* actions by the responsible political leaders of Canada and of other nations to lessen the effects of this

impending disaster seem to have been consistently too little or too late . . . [and]
whereas the growth of populations now makes the solution of a host of major political, social and individual problems more difficult and will eventually make satisfactory solutions impossible.

This tabled resolution concluded:

therefore, be it resolved that the C.S.W.F.B. voices its gravest concern to the Prime Minister of Canada, the Canadian Parliament, the Premiers of the ten provinces, officials at the other levels of government and to the people themselves, in the hope that they will assume immediately their responsibilities to take large-scale, effective and unprecedented action to curb population growth, by . . . [those] acts as may be needed to increase Canada's contribution to the realization of the larger goals of survival for the human species under acceptable conditions.

The C.S.W.F.B. President later reported in the Society's *Newsletter* (May 1971) that a substantial response, in the form of acknowledgements or favourable comments, was received. Only one response was negative: the M.P. for Edmonton West wrote that the C.S.W.F.B. "could more properly be concerned with matters dealing with wildlife and fishery biology rather than trying to moralize the question of population growth within the country."

Despite the apparently favourable reception of this appeal for action, it is impossible to gauge the real impact such lobbying makes on the national policy-making scene. But less than a month after this resolution was mailed to the Prime Minister, he was reported having said at a Vancouver meeting (1 May 1971) that "technological accomplishment and population growth have both reached such a rate of acceleration that the world at this moment is placed precariously at the commencement of several exponential curves. Going up at a perilous pace are population and pollution. . . . Isn't it time we paid heed to resource exhaustion, to environmental deterioration, to the social costs of overcrowding?"

The C.S.W.F.B. resolution called on the Chairman of the

Economic Council of Canada and the Chairman of the Science Council of Canada to have studies undertaken to ascertain the various implications of unplanned population growth, more especially for future generations of Canadians. The Science Council of Canada had already acknowledged the need for such studies, and in the *Chairman's Annual Report* for 1969–70 appears the statement: "Canada must soon set for itself a population goal for the future. This will not be easy but it is almost as important for Canada as for the more overcrowded countries" (Science Council of Canada 1970: 36).

A substantial strengthening of the pioneering attempts by the different scientists' groups to draw the governmental ostrich's head out of the sand came in the Science Council's next *Annual Report,* wherein about 60 per cent of the Chairman's statement is given over to urging national involvement with the question of a domestic population policy. The Chairman acknowledged the reasons why Canadians might at first be misled into believing their large country had no population problem, and then commented: "Nonetheless, nearly all the internal problems that concern us now would be much more manageable if our population growth were less rapid. Even in our vast country we must immediately begin to set goals for total population, rate of population growth and distribution of population" (Science Council 1971: 34).

Significantly also, in the 1971 report, the national goals proclaimed in the Science Council's 1968 report were subject to substantial revision: national prosperity, which ranked first of six goals in 1968, was last in 1971, with achievement of a stable and healthy environment the first goal.

A general awareness, not simply of population, but rather of the ecological perspective inherent in the population–environment–resources nexus of events, was stressed more and more in public utterances during 1971. For example, the President of the Canadian Institute of International Affairs warned that the essential issue for Canadians in the coming decades was to decide how to live with the international implications of our riches in a world increasingly occupied with the growing gap between population and resources (reported in Westell 1971).

A group of senior scientists working in Canadian universities and for industry and the government recently petitioned the

Prime Minister on the matter of governmental responsibility in the field of population goals and policy. Their letter stated in part:

> The task of limiting the size of Canada's human population and its pattern of resource use . . . is in our view the most urgent and awesome challenge of our time. The undoubted fact of its political sensitivity does nothing to diminish its reality or urgency: nor are Canadians one or two generations hence likely to view tolerantly our reluctance to deal resolutely with a problem that becomes more intractable with every day that it is left unrecognized. (Corbet and LeRoux 1972: 1.)

This letter was replied to by an Assistant Deputy Minister, Department of National Health and Welfare, who stated:

> There is, at present, no consensus in respect of, for example, the population problem in Canada . . . while he [Chairman of the Science Council of Canada] and you and many other scientists see the problem as one of overpopulation, others, including leading scientists, consider it a problem of underpopulation. (Corbet and LeRoux 1972: 32.)

This statement was answered by the group of concerned scientists, who offered an opinion as to the reasons for the alleged discrepancy between different scientists' viewpoints. They pointed out:

> Regarding the different viewpoints that are currently held concerning the nature of the population problem, our collective experience (which involves encounters with many scientists in Canada and elsewhere) leads us to conclude that, among those *whose special knowledge lies in the fields that are closely relevant to this question,* there is indeed a consensus that Canada's problem is one of over—rather than under population. (Corbet and LeRoux 1972; emphasis added.)

Meanwhile, although it does not appear at present that the government will initiate much direct action or public acknowledgement of the facts that concern more and more knowledgeable scientists whose competence lies near to the nub of the population question, the Science Council has decided to go ahead and institute a major study to investigate the vital role population plays in determining the type of life Canadians will likely be experiencing in the immediate future.

PEOPLE POLLUTION

Earlier I attempted to show that whatever the nature and principle cause of environmental stress, the addition of increasing numbers of people can only intensify and complicate the severity of the problem. Some authors go further and assert that growing numbers of people will before too long precipitate a situation so complex and extreme as to defy solution; in this view we may say that in unfettered reproduction we will sow the seeds of our own destruction!

Moreover, neither the numbers of people alone, nor even the density at which they live, are the principal cause of this global stress. It is when these large numbers are caught up in the now near-universal revolution of rising expectations and aspirations, with respect to material standards of existence, that intense and progressively damaging demands are placed on the environmental system which even today, according to most knowledgeable people, is dangerously near to the limit of continued viability. The analogy provided in the parable mentioned earlier in this chapter entitled *The 99th Hour* shows that, even if we are only half-way to the point of disaster, the terrible moment could be reached by just one more doubling of the stress—that is, at an unknown moment of time well within the present century. Some would say that we are more than half-way to that point of time.

Given the global nature of the problem, it clearly becomes irrelevant for us in Canada to pretend that we do not have a population problem; if the system goes we all go, and we certainly will not be able with any honesty to claim that we went blamelessly.

Personally I do not place that much weight upon the various piecemeal solutions which claim that indeed technology can, in the time available, either render our more abusive demands on the system innocuous, or give rise to miraculous and effective reforms in food production and distribution to keep alive the 3 to 4 million people who annually starve to death, to improve the diet of around 2,000 million undernourished and hungry people alive today, and to keep from the same fate the 50 million additional hungry bodies born each year.

For purposes of discussion, at least, I am willing to concede that the technical, intellectual, and economic resources do exist, and thereby offer a chance for continued survival of significant numbers of people for some time. The questions become: at what level of survival, and at what cost? For this reason the term "people pollution" becomes a pertinent concept, and has been described as, for example: "the consèquences, mental and physical, of life in a world vastly more populous and technologically more complex than the one in which we currently find ourselves. In such a world the goals of healthy and happy human beings, free from malnutrition, poverty, disease and war . . . [are likely to be] convincingly elusive" (Williamson 1969: 979).

To continue viewing the concept ecologically I would say that people pollution pertains when the size of the human population is greater than can be maintained indefinitely without detriment to the health of the individual from physiological, social, ideological, or aesthetic stress. We must acknowledge that this is a completely new problem faced by mankind, even though philosophers since Tertullian (or even before?) in the second century A.D. have observed man's increasing burdensomeness to nature. Indeed, as ecologist Eugene P. Odum has stated (1969), the basic problem today boils down to determining, in some objective way, when we are "getting too much of a good thing." "Too much," one commentator has observed, "exists if a person is forced to subject himself to the collectivity to such an extent that he loses essential individual attributes" (Querido 1964). The U.S. National Academy of Sciences has gone further in equating the implications of continued population growth with the threat posed, not to the individual, but to the species; they warn: "To delay progress toward self-regulation of population size is to play Russian roulette with the future of Man."

Chapter Five

CANADIAN POPULATION: THE ROOTS OF THE PROBLEM

Nature will neither be forced nor driven, and is often very hard to be led; but will do wonders when properly assisted.

THOMAS DOVER (1733)

The chief thing which differentiates man from the lower animals is an insatiable desire to abuse the human organism through wine, women and accidental self-destruction.

G. BERNARD (1855)

Nothing fails like success, because you do not learn anything from it. The only thing we ever learn from is failure. Success only confirms our superstitions.

KENNETH BOULDING (1970)

THE NATURE OF "NO-TECHNICAL-SOLUTION PROBLEMS"

Dr. Garrett Hardin, a biology professor at the University of California, has written a number of thought-provoking and incisive articles on the problems associated with population. In one of his most seminal articles, dealing with the roots and implications of overpopulation, Dr. Hardin notes that there exist classes of problems—for example, the nuclear arms race—for which there is probably no technical solution. Importantly also, seeking solutions to this class of problem in science and technology will worsen rather than alleviate or remove it. He goes on to write:

> The "population problem" as conventionally conceived, is a member of this class. . . . It is fair to say that most people who anguish over the population problem are trying to find a way to avoid the evils of overpopulation without relinquishing any of the privileges they now enjoy. They think that farming the seas or developing new strains of wheat will solve the problem—technologically. . . . The population problem cannot be solved in a technical way. (Hardin 1968b: 1243.)

Another senior biologist in the United States, Dr. Stanley Cain, has warned that the race between production and reproduction cannot be won by increasing production, and that moreover: "it seems to me to be fundamentally misleading for us to argue the problem from the science-based technology that man has created . . . what *can* be done is quite different from what *will* be done" (Cain 1967: 31).

What is evidently suggested here (and by many others concerned with this matter) as being primarily in need of revision and updating is our present value system and our attitudes, not the physical wherewithal to accomplish technologically certain definable objectives (see, for example, Huxley 1963).

Unfortunately, attitudes are less easy to remake than machines; however, for a constructive start, several commentators on environmental and population problems have sought to probe the ideological bases of our present dilemma. Some have seen the roots of current problems in the persistence of an uncurbed, unenlightened frontier mentality, so that to paraphrase the distinguished regional planner Ian McHarg, material gain is our measure, convenience is its cohort, the short term is its span, and the "devil take the hindmost" its morality.

This ethic basically views nature as being there solely to serve man's immediate acquisitive and expansive needs; it has its roots in much older beliefs wherein nature is the unredeemed setting for man's redemption, and in the Judeo-Christian story of creation, for example, which exhorts man "to be fruitful and multiply, fill the earth and subdue it, and have dominion over the fish of the sea and the birds of the air and over every living thing." Whether or not a literal interpretation of this text was intended, the message has clearly come through history that man is very fully licensed to subdue the earth, and, given the particular manner of Old Testament subjugation of the vanquished, the resulting treatment of conquered nature can come as no surprise.

Perhaps the strength of this doctrine to conquer nature stems not so much from the specifics of Judeo-Christian teaching *per se* as from a generalized implication inherent in monotheistic belief compared with the earlier widely prevalent and conflicting pantheistic and animistic religions with which the God of the early Israelites competed. The ensuing battle against this welter of false gods implied an all-out offensive against nature itself, which was not only the physical manifestation of the pantheistic creed but the stage upon which the empirical play of the animists was daily enacted. The new monotheism, in its turn, emphasized the relationship between man and a transcendental deity whose habitat was clearly not the lowly and profane earth.

These views have been challenged: for example, the biblical creation story is held by some Judaic and Christian scholars to be largely allegorical, and others (such as Barbour 1970) remind us that the Old Testament speaks of responsibility, respect, and stewardship of nature, and the essentially temporary trusteeship, by man, of the natural order. The continuing-creation philosophy of Jesuit Teilhard de Chardin also stresses the dependence, rather than dominance, theme of man–nature interrelationships, but such enlightened interpretations appear to have arrived too late to modify the ethical standards underlying collective conventional attitudes to the environment in those societies where, historically, "Western" religion has effected ideological conquest.

Interestingly, though equally unfortunately for modern man, the two major ideological power blocks in the modern world today both count as their heritage the influential philosophical views of Francis Bacon and of Hegel. Baconian views could have exerted a more ameliorative effect on man's interaction with nature, for the aphorism that we cannot command nature except by obeying her originates with Bacon. He also advocated that philosophy was not to remain as a teaching inactivity, but rather should seek creative invention for the purpose of changing and controlling nature in the service of human kind.

Karl Marx, whose ideological teachings powerfully underlie the governance of at least one-third of the human family, was profoundly influenced philosophically by Bacon, and by Hegel whose reflections on aesthetics at least leave no doubt that the works of man are to be considered superior to the works of nature. Thus Marx, and through him, the modern rulers of the Soviet and Chinese nations and their satellites adhere to the doctrine that man will produce a better society for himself by striving creatively to master nature (see Murphey 1967: 319 *ff.*, also Glacken 1970).

The reality of the matter is, however, that despite the underlying ideologies, North Americans among many others, whether morally influenced by rabbinical, Christian, or Marxist teachings, are increasingly aware of, and concerned about, a man-induced environmental crisis of progressively enlarging proportions. The practical dilemma is *not* that people perceive any newly arisen contradiction between traditional beliefs and current realities, but rather that individuals are not prepared to change their behaviour (even if grudgingly acknowledging the inappropriateness of that behaviour and the underlying value system), for this would demand their giving up privilege and possessions, amenities and attitudes which they hold dearly—with self-destroying fervour in fact.

VALUES, DECISIONS, AND THE ETHICAL PROCESS

A collection of people constituting a society require a coherent and collective set of mutually agreed-upon customary behaviours and attitudes in order to function adaptively and for the common good. This set of adaptive behaviours and sustaining attitudes comprises the culture of the group, and, in an evolutionary sense, constitutes their most potent ally in the survival equation. Societies and cultures evolve, however, for the same reason that populations and species evolve in the rest of nature, namely because constantly changing environmental conditions demand new adaptive strategies to ensure continuing survival.

Clearly the high value that man once placed on certain behaviour and attitudes may now, under changed (modern) conditions, have different adaptive value than when first incorporated into the cultural repertoire of the group. Indeed, some behaviour could conceivably be maladaptive to the point of threatening the well-being and ultimate survival of that particular society. Warfare might be one such outmoded behaviour, and the belief that the oceans can be viewed as a commons for exploiting resources or dumping our noxious effluents may be an example of an attitude of equal danger. What then is meant by saying "times have changed" when judging certain actions or thoughts inappropriate today? Undoubtedly many component parts of the total evaluative equation change through time; for example, there are more people alive today and they live in higher density settlements, their perceived needs are different, the technology at their disposal immeasureably advanced in effectiveness and power, and so on. In summary then, it would appear that in understanding what has "changed," we can identify three main areas, comprising: a demographic component (the population has grown and is subject to a different spatial arrangement); a technologic component (modern tools and techniques are highly efficacious); an ideological component (there is discordance not only between what we once wanted and now want, but, contemporaneously, to some extent also between what "we" want and what "they" want).

Owing to the complexity and heterogeneity of modern society it is doubtful if any more than a very small number of people will completely agree in all matters concerning reforms or changes for "good" or "bad." Today more than ever, perhaps, one man's meat is indeed another man's poison! Consider some of the main opposing factions in our society: government and opposition; labour and management; landlord and tenant; merchant and customer; developer and conservationist. The picture is far more complex than these simple dyadic representations suggest; for example, in a labour–management dispute the government is probably involved because of the political and economic repercussions of the outcome, other unions are similarly apprehensive, as are other industrial managements, and the public, as consumer, is usually involved directly (through strike action) or indirectly (through ensuing service, price, or tax changes). The interdependency and interlocking of component segments of any modern society are as complex and intricate as in any ecosystem in nature, and furthermore, tend to rise at a disproportionately accelerating rate relative to the increase in numbers of people in the system. The figures reproduced below indicate the numerical growth of functional relationships as an increasing number of individual workers are added to a management system.

NUMBER OF WORKERS	NUMBER OF POSSIBLE RELATIONSHIPS
1	1
2	6
3	18
4	44
5	100
6	222
7	490
8	1080
9	2376
10	5210

Present environmental issues illustrate as well as any matter can the problems inherent in resolving conflict of values produced by the heterogeneity of today's society. For example, setting up a new industrial plant or undertaking in a given area may be viewed negatively by local property owners, conservationists, and some national groups who may hold that the establishment detracts from the values they hold in high esteem; but the creation of jobs, financial return on an investment made, and future prospects of work nearby for local residents are equally valid justifications for encouraging the development in the view of other groups of people.

It is precisely because there exists, for different people, a different ordering of priorities and options that the choosing between alternatives becomes an ethical matter. I accept for present purposes Kenneth Boulding's statement that a moral or ethical proposition is a statement about a rank order of preferences among alternatives which is intended to apply to more than one person. This declaration becomes an ethical one when the position it represents implies or states explicitly that a particular choice or action *ought* to be taken, not just by the claimant, but by others as well. Thus ethical choice is different from mere personal preference, for individual tastes or styles are not held to be binding on others.

This small book is not intended to be a comprehensive examination of all or even some of the most important sociological and ecological aspects of environmental problems in Canada, but rather it attempts to focus more narrowly on the theme of people-problems associated with this complex issue. The remainder of the book therefore will attend more especially to probing the dilemma that appears to emerge when, in the name of the common good, certain painful decisions and choices have to be made. As the commitment and resolve to do something nationally and internationally must ultimately be a personal obligation by individuals, the burning question becomes, quite simply, just how much are we prepared to surrender and not just how much ought we to surrender. The decision is that much more difficult to answer honestly when it becomes apparent that what we must ultimately surrender includes certain basic freedoms presently held inviolate by many of us.

Tenacious as we are to preserve our basic freedoms, we may recognize at last that "something has to be done." To solve the population–environment problem philosophically merely requires that we establish what final values we intend to preserve. But we seek an actual, rather than a theoretical, solution to the question, and it is precisely because this constitutes an immeasurably harder task that the problem persists and, equally regrettably, precipitates an unconscionable refusal by many to even discuss the real issues involved.

As a prime example of avoidance of the real issues we might take the United Nations Conference on the Human Environment held in Stockholm in June 1972, after four years of preparatory discussion, consultation, and planning. An examination of the 800 pages of background material published prior to this greatest of all conferences to save the life-support system of this planet was far from reassuring. The basic philosophy on which the conference appeared to be built was that "we intend, by various technical means yet to be perfected, to have our cake, and eat it. What's more, even though *we* intend to keep it *and* eat it, *you* can have it too!" Of the four main factors generally recognized to be at the root of the present global environmental crisis, namely, population, pollution, the unequal distribution of consumption, and the depletion of non-renewable resources, only one was treated in any detail. I am not sure which is the more significant observation to make, that the one factor discussed at length, namely pollution, is the most amenable to solution by means of technological fixes (though not wholly so of course), or that three of the four root causes for major environmental stress to all intents and purposes remained largely unmentioned. With respect to the conference objectives, Canada's stated position was published two months before the June meeting, and it characteristically accorded with the international good-neighbour principle by strictly avoiding mention of the sensitive real problems.

For the sake of argument, let us assume that we are going to look objectively at the situation, either as intensely rational people or because we finally *are* convinced that we need to come to grips with the extant problem. If the solution depends, as mentioned earlier, on determining what ultimate values we intend to preserve, we need to establish not only certain goals but also the means by which these are to be served. Goals are of two main types for any society at any period in time, namely, proximate and ultimate.

Proximate goals will vary according to the circumstances of the particular society, or sector of that society, pertaining at that moment in its history. Thus, for example, in the underdeveloped Canadian north or parts of the Maritime provinces today, examples of legitimate proximate goals might be an accelerated rate of, or increased degree of, industrial expansion, or adoption of policies favouring private investment of other sorts. On the other hand, in the more fully industrialized regions of Canada, proximate goals might more properly be concerned with improving the quality of life by barring further industrial activity, or returning some areas to the public domain for recreational use.

Despite the disparate objectives and sectional appeal of proximate goals, ultimate goals on the other hand enjoy more nearly universal appeal, for example, increasing or maintaining security, knowledge, justice, freedom.

The definition of ethics suggested earlier requires that these various goals be ranked; this is, to be sure, an infinitely more troublesome task than merely listing them! In a comprehensive study entitled *Ethics and Population Limitation,* the director of the Institute of Society, Ethics, and the Life Sciences in New York has observed that three values appear to play a predominant role in Western society, namely freedom, justice, and security-survival; he then asks: "How much procreative freedom, if any, should be given up in order to ensure the security-survival of a nation or a community? . . . How much procreative freedom can be tolerated if it jeopardizes distributive justice?" (Callahan 1972: 489).

As if these questions are not hard enough to answer as they stand, there is also the overriding question: "How much *certainty* of the outcome or need must be possessed before the right exists to *demand* compliance to new standards of conduct?"

THE QUESTION OF FREEDOM

Increased freedom should bring increased collective awareness, responsibility, and ultimately well-being, but all too often it precipitates an individual recklessness that threatens to eventually destroy the freedom of others even to exist. Professor Garret Hardin's paper (1968b) "The Tragedy of the Commons" argues this point, namely the pervasive danger inherent in a relentless pursuit of maximizing the value accorded individual freedom. As a paradigm of man's present predicament, caused by stressing fully the ethic of unbridled growth in a finite world, the dramatic tragedy bears repeating.

We are asked to consider a pasture, open to all herdsmen. As individual ownership of cattle, and hence individual profit, is dependent upon sufficiency of pasture for one's cattle, it is in any manager's immediate best interest to keep as many cattle as he can on the commons. As a rational man the herdsman will try to maximize his gain, but also as a rational man he may recognize a cost as well as a benefit resulting from the additional cattle he adds to the range.

The benefit to the individual herdsman of one more head of cattle is the profit resulting from this addition; as he takes all the profit from this increment, the gain in utility to him is $+1$.

The cost, on the other hand, is a function of the overgrazing caused by an additional animal on the commons. The deficit is not borne by the one herdsman alone, however, but by all those using the commons. Thus his loss is only a fraction of -1.

Solving this cost–benefit analysis leads to the conclusion that the net gain makes it worthwhile adding to his herd. This same decision, however, has been reached by every other rational herdsman sharing the commons. Therein lies the tragedy, for each man is locked into a system that compels him to increase the size of his estate without limit in a world that is, indeed, limited. The inevitable outcome of this drama is ruin for all, the ultimate path for any society wherein its members, in the name of freedom, are allowed to pursue, unrestrained, their own best interest in the face of limited resources.

The escape from this dangerous and inexorable pathway to ruin comes, according to Professor Hardin, in recognizing that as man's population size and density increases so the commons mentality must be superseded by instituting generally acceptable restrictions on certain individual freedoms. As an example, we note that when cars were in limited numbers one could park a car virtually anywhere, whereas today in areas of high car density we accept the need for strict controls on parking, from mild discouragement in the form of metered areas exacting a financial penalty to areas totally prohibiting parking. It is important to realize that these restrictions represent infringements on the personal freedom of some members of society (as do disqualifications from driving handed down by the courts), but society as a whole does not now condemn, far less prohibit, such violations of individual freedom. The reason for condoning restrictive legislation is because its enactment under certain specified circumstances enables many more people to experience continued freedom and enhanced enjoyment and fulfilment.

Freedom, therefore, comes from the recognition of necessity by the majority, rather than through lack of restriction placed on individual maximization, though seemingly the maturity that allows expression to that freedom is rarely gained without benefit of serious inconvenience or bitter experience. I am reminded of the timeless words a Canadian Eskimo shaman spoke to the Danish explorer-anthropologist, Dr. Knud Rasmussen: "All true wisdom is to be found far from the dwellings of men . . . and can only be attained through suffering and privation. Suffering and privation are the only means that open the minds of men to that which is hidden from their fellows."

At this point in human history we need to ask: how much collective suffering is necessary before we can accept the need for restrictions placed on our liberty to act in certain spheres of activity? Furthermore, given the time lag between our realization that something may indeed be wrong and the sudden resolve to do something about it, can we act in a sufficiently purposive and effective manner to right the particularly stressful condition that appears as one major root of our problem? According to some (for example, eminent economist Joseph Spengler), a conflict of freedoms is at the root of the population problem. The individual licence to procreate appears to have run head-on into a variety of freedoms the remainder of society wish to enjoy, a conflict caused because the externalities of excessive child-bearing are now increasingly borne by other members of society (Spengler 1969).

THE EVOLUTIONARY BASIS OF POTENTIAL HUMAN OVERPRODUCTION

An important evolutionary development leading to the human condition was the removal of sex from a purely reproductive function to that of powerful influence in social affairs. The evolutionary rise of modern man has, to be sure, included many important steps forward, but undoubtedly the onset of the family as a basic social unit, rather than the troupe or horde as in other ecologically similar primates, was a vitally important prerequisite for the further development and transmission of culture.

The family, consisting basically of an adult male, his spouse(s), and at least some of their offspring, requires a very powerfully attractive bond to remain together through sufficient time to prepare the offspring for independent social life. Man, the only mammal having lost the restricted cyclical nature of sexual receptiveness, makes use of this constancy of sexual desire to forge that bond between individual male and female.

The reason for this apparent digression into physical anthropology is because human sexuality, the physical basis of our reproductive tendencies, in some sectors of our society continues to be viewed as a very modern awakening, somehow the result of recently changed standards of conduct and morality. On the contrary, many cultures and societies, whether tribal or at various stages of modernity, acknowledge the basic and powerful force of unrestrained human sexuality and its potential danger to the social order. The containment of this possible hazard is by powerful social and cultural institutions, but, being man-made and therefore subject to human rationality and variability, such controlling institutions can and do change through time without necessarily bringing the society in question down in ruins.

The social, as opposed to merely reproductive, function of human sexuality can be adduced from the removal of this essential and basic human behaviour from the confines of purely involuntary control, where it most certainly would be expected to remain if serving a solely reproductive function. In fact, the increasing cortical (mental) control of sexual and reproductive activity facilitates the development of certain culturally acceptable, though biologically aberrant, voluntary behaviours such as, for example, celibacy. It remains to be seen, however, whether the ability to further rationalize human sexuality can become widely and quickly enough dispersed to save man from the threats posed by his overproductive technological and reproductive proclivities. As University of California demographer

Judith Blake (1971: 215) has warned: "If we take our reproductive institutions as given, even as sacrosanct, we give up our primary basis for orderly demographic adaptation." The concluding chapters will consider some measures that might be taken to effect such an orderly demographic adaptation.

RELEVANCE OF ABORTION

It is useful to consider some aspects of the abortion issue, not because at some point in time during the secular development of the nation the issue cannot be avoided further, but because at this time the antagonists in the debate are about as far apart on some issues as are more extreme conservation and "boomer" groups with respect to environmental issues. The problems of abortion and of environment–population rationalization have other similarities: for example, both deal with the question of alleged inalienable rights, and the thorny issue of changing the hitherto sacrosanct values that gave force to those rights. There is another, more subtle, relationship pointed out by Harvard Divinity School professor, Ralph B. Potter, Jr. (1971: 107), who writes: "When a fetus is aborted no one asks for whom the bell tolls. No bell is tolled. But do not feel indifferent and secure. The fetus symbolizes you and me and our tenuous hold upon a future here at the mercy of our fellow men."

With regard to the hopes for an eventual solution to the abortion problem, we hold as many factually unsound and sociologically naïve opinions as we do about the piecemeal solution of our environmental–population complex of problems. For example, how many times are we advised that sex education in the schools and a network of family-planning clinics and the easy availability of effective contraceptives will stop the demand for abortion? Will it? What of the enlightened Scandinavian countries, so often held up as shining examples of what we should do; do they have no illegitimate or unwanted children, no illegal abortion? On the contrary, despite the development, over thirty years, of what is generally considered to be a model and humane approach to unwanted pregnancy and sex education, Sweden, for example, still has not only a persistent illegal abortion problem but a flow of Swedish women seeking abortions in Britain and Poland (see Ottosson 1971).

The reasons for this seemingly puzzling behaviour have been explained elsewhere (Freeman 1970: 145-46), but here we might just observe that this lesson should serve as a reminder that firstly, there are no simple and obvious social, educational, or technological solutions to some classes of human problems. Secondly, it appears that, despite the best will in the world, it may nevertheless take decades to effect solutions to such problems even when we expend great efforts to seek that end. Our problem here in Canada is confounded by the fact that we do not have prevailing the best will in the world to seek such solutions, and, further, that we have not yet *started* on the road to effective action, and in many instances have not even begun to *discuss* with honesty and frankness the nature of the problems, far less the solutions. Just how far have we progressed since the time, a few short years ago, when the word abortion was taboo and the euphemism "illegal operation" was all that correct North American society allowed reference to?

In June 1969 certain amendments to the Canadian Criminal Code were enacted with the purpose of specifying under what circumstances therapeutic abortions could be lawfully performed in Canadian hospitals. In retrospect, the passage of these amendments is seen by one Royal Commission and several scholarly studies (for example, see references in Veevers 1971) to be a rather inept effort to liberalize some inappropriate legislation without in fact achieving that desired goal. The debate in the Canadian Parliament, moreover, indicated the extent of the vocal opposition still remaining: for example, the Creditiste member for Shefford, P.Q., was reported to have said that the proposed reforms were "to give more freedom to the depraved people in this country, and to please the easy-going women of our society who could not care less about their neighbors and our race. It is also to please credulous girls who fall easily into the gutter and also to please flighty ones who go out night after night to conquer new lovers, and also to please dissipated women who lack foresight."

Clearly the new changes in the law were meeting with opposition from both sides of the debate; however, in May 1970 a number of significant events gave physical expression to the growing sentiment in Canada favouring further reforms. The new laws were very plainly not allowing the intent of the reforms to be realized, namely, to make a legal termination of pregnancy available to *all* Canadians whose health would be endangered by carrying a pregnancy to term. Starting in British Columbia, where the Vancouver Women's Caucus had operated a counselling and abortion referral service for some time, a series of meetings and campaigns were held in a number of Canadian cities en route to Ottawa. In a few weeks this group had made itself noticed, through speeches in the House of Commons, challenging the Prime Minister and federal Ministers of Justice and of Health and Welfare at public meetings, and presenting briefs to such bodies as the Canadian Medical Association and the Canadian Psychiatric Association. More than any other similar body, this caucus served to unite into an articulate pressure group women from a great diversity of social, economic, political, and geographic segments of Canada (Maeots 1970: 157).

September 1970 saw a number of significant events that added visible support to the movement calling for reform; the respectable and widely read women's magazine *Chatelaine* editorialized on the injustices inherent in the present abortion laws, and *Maclean's Magazine* gave national prominence to the anguish of a married, middle-class Canadian woman who "went through hell for a legal abortion." Even more momentous, however, was the appearance in September 1970 of the *Report of the Royal Commission on the Status of Women* which, after stating that the present abortion laws were bad, included among its recommendations that abortion on request be permitted in the first twelve weeks of pregnancy, and thereafter under certain specified medical circumstances. This view, favouring a more liberal approach to abortion, appeared to reflect a majority of Canadians' thoughts on the subject (see, for example, C.B.C. National Poll, 1971: 15); more germane to our present discussion, however, was the guiding principle which appeared to influence one of the dissenting Commissioners, University of Montreal demographer Dr. Jacques Henripin. The minority report by Dr. Henripin drew attention to the fundamental position, basic to the Western ethical system, taken by the opponents to liberal abortion laws: namely, the respect for human life.

The ethic respecting human life is a common denominator of all opinions expressed in the abortion debate, from the reforming left-wing to the conservative right-wing. With some commonality of viewpoint it is to be hoped that resolution of opposing beliefs might in time be possible; if some measure of agreement is reachable, then hope remains that certain important questions seemingly preventing the formulation and enactment of population policies will likewise appear more soluble. The following section does not attempt to judge or to resolve the present abortion conflict, but rather to report certain implications of the present difficulty and, more especially, to make explicit the limitation of reason alone in reconciling opposing views held in areas where no recourse can be made to scientific or objective facts.

ABORTION: WHAT'S AT STAKE, REALLY?

A comprehensive national opinion poll conducted by the Canadian Broadcasting Corporation (1971) indicated that though a majority of Canadians, 18 years of age and over, feel that present abortion laws are too restrictive, only about one-quarter of the population advocate abortion on request, and only 5 per cent believe abortion should be strictly prohibited. Thus we might conclude that, despite their vociferousness, the two extremes of the spectrum of opinions regarding abortion—namely, abortion on request and no abortion—still represent, at this time, a minority viewpoint.

Social norms and political action tend to follow the views of the majority rather than the minority, so for purposes of discussion here I intend to examine the basis of this moderate viewpoint (aforementioned poll result), which represents a majority Protestant perspective. The reader interested in the right-wing, Catholic, viewpoint is referred to essays by, for example, St. John-Stevas and Wassmer, in Hardin 1969.

The most cogent recent discussions of the Protestant viewpoint on abortion are contained in the writings (particulary 1967) of Dr. Ralph B. Potter, Jr., Professor of Social Ethics at Harvard Divinity School; the interpretation below relies heavily on one such essay (1971). See also Dr. Potter's recent book (1969) entitled *Updating Life and Death,* for further discussion of the topic.

It is apparent that in modern society, as part of the progressive secularization of beliefs, theological certitude gives way to individual responsibility for deciding moral conduct; individual conscience, rather than divine judgement, has become the proximate sanction for ensuring appropriate personal behaviour. Included in this changed outlook is the realization that pregnancy frequently results from human improvidence, including unintended contraceptive failure, rather than some divine act of providence.

When in good conscience and according to God-given rational powers a couple decide to deliberately limit their fertility, the refusal even to consider the possibility of utilizing abortion when it is presented as an available option becomes a partial denial of their new-found rationality and desire to consciously control their own destiny. Thus, one Anglican minister recently observed that a sense of responsibility is of paramount importance in parenthood; proper birth control and family planning are now accepted as a demonstration of both responsibility and respect. He suggests that, just as reasonably, judicious, concerned use of abortion can be an act of responsible parenthood and moral respect (McLennan 1972: 15). Even where the individual finds, for aesthetic if not moral reasons, some reluctance in exercising this particular option, to deny others the freedom to do so, if they choose, is seen to constitute a violation of another's rights to self-determination.

This trend of thought is strengthened by the realization, not too widespread at present, that the alternatives are not between abortion and contraception, but between abortion and compulsory pregnancy; few people will contemplate abortion unless they are already pregnant, at which time, of course, contraception is beside the point (see Hardin 1968a).

The fact that the middle-of-the-road majority, although accepting abortion, have nevertheless chosen to reject the ultimate freedom of abortion on request indicates that what they espouse is not an unqualified acceptance of the operation, but rather the validity of *justifiable* abortion. These moderates, however, will necessarily disagree on what constitutes justification, for to most people abortion remains a troubling issue with several ethical questions remaining unanswered.

The further one moves to the left, the more the force of the argument depends upon primary stress being placed on the moral right to self-determination. The right wing counters this by emphasizing the rights of the fetus. If the right wing concedes that the fetus only represents *potential* human existence, but, being human, necessarily requires respect and protection, the left will counter with the rights of the mother (and her family) to respect and protection enabling realization of her (their) unfulfilled potential.

Without going further into the specifics of the conflict, the following dichotomy in values becomes apparent, a dichotomy which has pertinence to the ethical questions raised by population-policy advocates who stress the need for public fertility-control programs. The left wing (abortion reform group) stresses: the right of self-determination; primacy of the rights of the born over the unborn. The right wing (anti-abortion group) emphasizes: primacy of group over individual well-being; high value on the human potential of the unborn. Interestingly, although the advocates of a national population policy generally accord to the left in respect to the abortion issue, their advocacy implicitly includes values embraced by the right-wing group in that same abortion debate, namely: primacy of the common good at the expense of individual goal seeking; high value on protecting the interests of future generations from the selfish behaviour of today's generation.

To conclude this excursion into controversy, I would merely stress certain implications of the issues both involved in the abortion debate and also pertinent to the environmental crisis in Canada as I see it. Firstly, controversies rarely disappear on their own, but generally require frank and full discussion by knowledgeable and concerned people. There is very little written or researched on non-medical aspects of abortion in Canada (however, see Pelrine 1971), so the knowledge required to seek resolution may yet be absent even if the concern is real enough. This is particularly unfortunate because in the absence of pertinent new information positions presently taken may harden into intractability, with a real danger that failure to clarify the abortion issue may impede implementation of fertility-control programs that rely on effective voluntary means of birth control. The reason for that conclusion is twofold. Firstly, any family-planning program, whether private or public, seeks to establish and/or maintain a high level of contraceptive motivation. The ultimate goal sought, however, is not contraception *per se* but rather avoidance of the consequences of unwanted pregnancy. When contraception fails—and the best methods in common use today still have a 1 per cent failure rate (resulting in Canada in about 30,000 unplanned pregnancies per year)—the strong desire to avoid having a child will probably persist. This inclination rises with age and number of children already produced so, although surgical sterilization is often resorted to subsequently, there does remain the residual problem of people who view giving up their child for possible adoption as a greater evil than therapeutic termination of their pregnancy. The present number of abortions in Canada and on Canadian women who go abroad to obtain the operation is unknown; estimates range widely but the Royal Commission on the Status of Women in attempting to evaluate the figures suggested 100,000 illegal abortions per year; about 5,000 women go from Canada to New York State alone each year, for legal surgery, and 31,000 legal abortions were registered in Canada in 1971.

Recognizing the failure of contraception to prevent all unwanted pregnancies, abortion is generally considered to be a necessary component of comprehensive birth-control programs. Indeed, in several national and state programs contraceptive failure is considered legitimate grounds for therapeutic termination of the ensuing unwanted pregnancy (Eliot 1967: 49). It appears likely that if that were not so, the program would be compromised in its stated goals: if people could not get the measure of control over fertility they were led to believe existed, some loss of program credibility would ensue. Continuing high motivation of users naturally depends upon sustained public trust.

The second reason for regretting the non-resolution of abortion controversies is related to the fact that one-method fertility-control programs are known to be less successful than multi-method programs (see, for example, Robert G. Potter 1971, 1972); some of the more promising methods of contraception (including intra-uterine devices, contra-gestational and anti-zygotic oral preparations) are thought to be, at least in part, abortifacient in action (Segal and Tietze 1971). Thus, the "morning-after pill" will pose no ethical dilemma for most people wishing to avoid pregnancy. The likelihood remains, however, that a conservative minority can continue to invoke human costs by keeping alive as political issues absolutist systems of morality which maintain, on theological grounds alone, that human life has full meaning from the moment egg and sperm conjoin. The social origins of that theological opinion should be well remembered, for in earlier times when survivability was low and abortion was the commonest form of birth control, the Church as well as the State needed the physical presence of every individual who could be produced; thus: "There was a convenient alliance of secular nationalism and ecclesiastical natalism. The moral evil of abortion was also a social evil which would deny the state a citizen, a soldier, a producer" (Ralph B. Potter 1971: 99).

The needs of the state may now be better served by a reversal of the conservative ecclesiastical pronatal policies of the early Church. Most Protestant churches have now accepted the contraceptive implications of responsible parenthood, and in most instances stand with the majority in conceding the value inherent in justifiable abortion. The short-term hope must be that the conservative churches will, at the very least, be moved by a growing ecumenical spirit of Christian charity not to impede the legitimate aspirations of the majority to live their lives within secular law according to the dictates of their individual consciences, and will recognize also that, though they have at present the opportunity (through politicians' temerity) to impose their ethics on the whole of society, they properly have only the right of moral persuasion (McLennan 1972: 6).

To paraphrase Professor Potter once more, for the right wing an entire system of meaning might be at stake in the abortion debate . . . but is anything less at stake for a secular, pluralistic state?

Chapter Six

POPULATION POLICY AND NORMATIVE BEHAVIOUR

A major excuse for the Canadian government not initiating any public discussion concerning the need for a comprehensive population policy is that, as of September 1970, it had embarked upon a program of information, training, and research in family planning; services, in the form of cost-sharing programs established by provincial and municipal agencies, began to get underway shortly thereafter. In some way, therefore, the government appears to equate family planning with population policy, as in the following statement in a recent document, produced by the Department of National Health and Welfare, entitled *Current Status of Family Planning in Canada*: "Family planning must also be considered in its global context. The resources of the world are finite and if population growth remains unchecked, these resources will not stretch to meet the needs of future generations." Specifically referring to Canada, this document points out:

Although birth rates have been declining since 1957, Canada's population doubled between 1933 and 1969, and forecasters predict that it will double again in about 35 years. Combined with increasing urbanization, this population places a tremendous burden on existing facilities and resources, and imposes physical and emotional stresses on the people involved. It therefore becomes increasingly necessary to ensure that family planning services are available to all citizens who desire them.

This support of family-planning programs, as desirable as it is long overdue, can in no way be considered a substitute for, nor even a major component of, a comprehensive population policy, for the following reasons.

Firstly, the major premise and goal of the planned-parenthood/family-planning movement is that every child should be a wanted child. Admirable as an ideal, this is in fact potentially disastrous, as it stands, for the wanting of six or eight children by some parents bears no relation to the realistic ability (or inability) of the parents, society, or the environment to absorb that size of population increment. Thus the ideal, though ostensibly in the short-run working in the interests of the family, can, also in the short-run, work against the good of society and ultimately therefore against the good of families, including those the program sets out to serve.

Secondly, the public and private programs supported by government are based on the assumption that significant numbers of people want fewer children, or want to space their children intelligently, but lack the financial, informational, and/or technical wherewithal to accomplish this end. There is little reliable evidence to support this belief, however, and such as does exist suggests rather powerfully that the majority of people in our type of society who desire to restrict their fertility do so fairly effectively, and that those who persist in their high fertility behaviour, for the most part, do so because they either positively favour having a large family or, more likely, place low value on contraception (see, for example, Blake 1969, for a review of this subject). Indeed, there is some likelihood that, with persistent norms favouring large families, the advent of benefits derived from family-planning activities will positively influence couples to *persist* in their desires to have large families by alleviating the desperate physical or economic conditions (a frequent outcome of too many children too soon) that otherwise might cause them to limit their offspring. Reasons such as these have caused one commentator to perceive an ecological parallel between family planning and DDT: twenty-five years ago both were important breakthroughs promising a safer and better life for all; now, however, both have backfired, threatening to destroy what they have helped to create (Chasteen 1972: 75).

There can be no argument with the professed concern of the government that fertility control remain a voluntary program. In rejecting the notion of coercion or compulsion one is led to the alternative of education. We must remember, however, that initiatives not now seized represent compounded problems twenty years hence, seriously reducing our available options at that date, so that our educational programs will, necessarily, have to be very effective. They will require a vigour, an uncompromising exposure of the implications of the *status quo* or reform, such that citizens will wish to seriously re-examine certain personal attitudes. We are not speaking of compulsion here, merely of government assurance that the Canadian people as a whole are exposed to factual information pertinent to our present collective circumstances. If some provinces or educational authorities claim infringement of their constitutional rights to handle this their own way, then, rather than acquiesce, the government has a duty to the Canadian nation to seek amendments to an outmoded constitution.

What we are really speaking of, when we mention population policy, are concerns larger than those of the individual family although of significance to it. To quote again from the government report on the *Current Status of Family Planning in Canada,* p. 6, population policy must be comprehensive enough to recognize, and work to overcome, such matters as:

> Problems of inadequate housing, hospitals, schools, jobs, transportation and recreation [which] are all in part caused by excessive population growth. Not least is the inescapable reduction of personal freedom—loss of dignity, personal value and identity due to excess population concentration.

What we now see in Canada is not very encouraging: a piecemeal approach that naïvely seeks solution to human ecological problems by attention to arbitrarily defined sub-sets of the complex of interrelated matters. Thus we have task forces on housing, a search for a national urban policy, programs to treat regional disparity, family planning, incomes and wages, and so on. A host of different agencies, different ministers and staffs, all working within rather rigorously defined bureaucratic boundaries. Such an approach to social problem-solving augers poorly for eventual framing of any population policy, for it seems likely that any plan that aims to reduce fertility by altering ideals concerning family size must do it through attention to diverse means; some examples include: increasing female participation and mobility in careers outside of the home, reducing certain non-economic benefits at present associated with having children (by allowing access to such benefits by other means), and generally re-ordering our social environment so that satisfying and rewarding human relationships exist outside of the family. For such reasons population policy must necessarily be comprehensive in scope, and be seen to contribute significantly toward an increase in the quality of life.

STABILIZING POPULATION BY ELIMINATING UNWANTED PREGNANCY

There can be no doubt at all that, in human terms, the elimination of unwanted pregnancy by appropriate use of the perfect contraceptive would be of enormous social value. At the present time of course, we have neither the perfect contraceptive device nor any means of ensuring either its effective dissemination or its widespread acceptibility. It seems very likely that the search for such a means of fertility control will continue to be made, and that considerably more acceptance of the value of birth control will be apparent to more and more people. We might then ask just how realistic is it to hope that population might be stabilized by merely averting the birth of all unplanned and unwanted children?

A recent study in the United States concluded that, in fact, preventing the population increment at present resulting from "unwanted pregnancy" would contribute significantly to the ultimate goal, for that nation, of Zero Population Growth. The assumptions entering into this calculation were that the sum of illegitimate births, legal abortions, and estimated totals of women unsuccessfully seeking abortions (both legal and illegal) would give the total number of unwanted pregnancies (Bumpass and Westoff 1970; their conclusion is supported by some other demographers, for example Coale 1970: 136).

In Britain, the size of the annual birth increment and the rate of population growth is much smaller than in the United States. Various evidence was obtained from hospital maternity wards, showing: about 50 per cent of pregnancies were reported to be unplanned, the incidence of illegitimate births was 24 per cent, the legitimized births nevertheless conceived out of wedlock amounted to 28 per cent, and a current high rate of applications for legal abortion. Medical researcher Sir Alan Parkes, using these data, has concluded (1970) that elimination of "unwanted" children would go far toward stabilizing the population of the United Kingdom, a judgement shared by some social reformers and sociologists in that country (for example, Simms and Medawar 1970, G. P. Hawthorn 1960b).

A recent study in the United States, however, has drawn a completely opposite conclusion, namely, that elimination of unwanted births occurring at present would, in fact, do little to assist in stabilizing the population of that nation (Blake 1971). Furthermore, the demographer responsible for this latter study believes that the assertion that Zero Population Growth can result from better and more accessible means of birth control is at this time an article of faith rather than scientific fact.

The American study by Bumpass and Westoff (1970) had earlier drawn a conclusion, similar to the British study, that was made conditional: that is, the elimination of unwanted births would lead to a reduced growth rate for the United States *only if there was no marked increase in the number of children desired per family.* In fact, the authors concluded that it remained of prime importance to influence people to desire, and hopefully thereby have, fewer children, though they believed that the elimination of unwanted births might be an easier goal to attain than influencing ideals about desirable family size.

The reasons for having children when and in the numbers

they are desired is knowledge of prime importance for purposes of formulating population policy, or even for designing comprehensive family-planning programs. It is regrettable that at this time very little is known about the sociological and psychological aspects of "planning" or "wanting" babies. The values a society holds, including those lumped together as "morals," are subject to continual change, as is well known, and it is as wrong to conclude (as some demographic studies unfortunately do) that all pregnancies occurring outside of marriage are unplanned, just as it is erroneous to believe that all unplanned pregnancies lead to unwanted children. In trying to evaluate these studies, then, we are handicapped by lack of adequate background information of a very fundamental nature. It would appear that we are not much further on now than a decade ago when a Cornell University demographer, Dr. J. Mayone Stycos, observed that we appear to know more about what people expect, want, and do with respect to planting wheat or purchasing TV sets than to having babies.

Considering therefore that there does not exist pertinent factual information on which to base an unequivocable answer to the question "whether Canada could stabilize its population by elimination of unwanted births," I must conclude that there are no grounds for an optimistic prognosis either. It is not necessary to refer to actual numbers, for the relative trends give a clear enough picture. For example, in Britain, it has been concluded that elimination of unwanted births would "go far toward" reducing the population growth rate of that country. But Britain is a country with a rate of illegitimate births more than twice that of Canada, even though we might suppose that freer access to abortion in Britain would have produced a lower number. In addition, Canada's rate of population growth is about double that of Britain, so an even greater degree of birth reduction would be required in this country even to approach the condition of "going far toward" stabilizing population.

The United States figures do nothing to brighten the prognosis, for both the illegitimacy rate and overall population growth rate are nearer to British than to Canadian levels. If Professor Judith Blake's criticism of the earlier American study is valid, as seems quite likely, in part if not *in toto,* it is equally applicable to the British data and conclusions, and thus we may infer that elimination of so-called "unwanted" births, under present circumstances, is most unlikely to contribute in any significant manner to the goal of a stable population.

THE SMALL FAMILY NORM: DEMOGRAPHIC CONSIDERATIONS

Although in Canada there is a downward trend in average family size, there is no doubt that, at its present slow rate of decrease, our current fertility behaviour guarantees to our children that population-aggravated environmental problems will inexorably increase until controls of one sort or another are inevitably forced upon them by the inherited condition of their times.

If their inheritance bothers us very much, we might decide to encourage people to have fewer children, for those children's sake if not for our own future well-being. How likely is it, from what is known of current population trends, that Canadians will adopt the norm of smaller family size, perhaps in the direction of two, rather than three children as at present? Before looking at whatever evidence we do have, it should be stressed that a statistical figure of about two children per couple does not mean that no one can have more than two children, for many couples may decide that they want only one child, or may choose to have larger families by adopting one or several children. Furthermore, at present levels of medical research it appears that from 8 to 10 per cent of all couples will remain either infertile or sub-fecund so that they will continue to find it physiologically impossible to produce children of their own.

Comprehensive studies of Canadian fertility (for example, Henripin 1968, Légaré and Henripin 1971) suggest that the probable completed-family size of this current generation of women aged 30-39 years will be in the range of 3.25 to 3.5 children per family; a decade earlier, when completed-family size of the same-aged women was about 3.5, only about 12.5 per cent of married women had a one-child family and only 9 per cent had no children. Performance, however, does not necessarily correspond to prevailing attitudes with respect to the "desired" family size; we would certainly expect that many of the women in the one-child and childless categories would have preferred larger families, but were frustrated in their desires by either their or their spouse's medical incapacity, or widowhood, divorce, or other unforeseen and regretted circumstances.

The following four observations tend to support the notion that prevailing attitudes still favour larger, rather than smaller, family size as being ideal. Firstly, a national survey in the United States (where, as in Canada, completed-family size is about three) found that in 1970 only 7 out of 1334 respondents desired a one-child family, and even fewer opted for childlessness in marriage (Blake 1971: 216). Secondly, the York University Family Study recently conducted among university students in Toronto indicated a range of ideal number of children from 2.5 to 3.7, tending once again to cluster near an average value of 3 (Simmons 1971). Thirdly, a recent analysis of the demographic bases of Canadian society has indicated that whereas percentages of families with zero, one, and two children fell progressively in each of the years 1941, 1951, 1961, and 1966 (data from the 1971 census being unavailable), percentages of families with three, four, and five children rose during the same period. Significantly, also, the study noted that the largest proportionate increases have occurred in families with three and four children (Kalbach and McVey 1971: 295). Lastly, noting that several recent changes are apparent in the fertility data obtained from Canadian vital statistics over the past decade, one comprehensive analysis has concluded that declines can be explained not by reduction in family size but rather by a change in timing of childbirth, so that when these *postponements* are over fertility rates will probably recover (Légaré and Henripin 1971: 116; see also *Canada Yearbook* 1970–71: 298).

It is true that crude birth rates in Canada are declining: 28.0 births per 1000 population in 1955, 27.3 in 1959, 21.1 in 1965, and 17.6 in 1969. But this is a misleading statistic for a variety of reasons, some of which have already been discussed (see Chapter 4). Therefore, apart from the various sound demographic reasons for not taking heart from a numerically decreasing measure of crude birth rate, we should also note well one salient sociological factor. The decision by a proportion of a given year's newly married couples to delay producing their first child can, in a young population such as Canada's, change the birth-rate without in any significant way affecting the ultimate growth increment those couples will add *unless* they defer permanently their desire to have certain additional children.

Thus, as in Bumpass and Westoff's study (1970), the conclusion is reached again that family size is an especially crucial variable. If fewer family formations take place and no great increase in births outside of marriage occurs, then net reproductive rate could fall without any change in average completed family size. Evidence suggests, however, that, despite rising divorce rate, marriage and remarriage rates remain high and thus we cannot look to increasing childlessness through non-marriage as a practical means of reducing the positive increment to national population growth. About 100,000 new marriages occur each year, and the number is forecast to rise to 150,000 annually by the end of the present decade. In absolute terms this represents 6.34 million families in 1980, compared with 4.57 million in 1966. With an additional 100,000 or more new families each year licensed to procreate, the elimination of the 33,000 illegitimate births annually, even if remotely possible, does not seem to hold the answer for stabilizing population.

Clearly then, family size must be reduced if net reproductive rate is to approach 1.0, that is, the replacement rate. For that to occur, given the demographic characteristics of the present Canadian population, an average of about 2.3 children per family would be required. Though this figure is the same as the 2.3 children per family average pertaining in Canada today, this latter number refers to the average of all families now existing, the largest single component of which are new, and as yet childless, families. The goal of 2.3 must refer to average *completed-*family size, which at the present time stands at more than 3.3. Under prevailing rates of decrease in family size occurring in Canada, 2.3 children per completed family will probably not be reached until the children born in 1972 finish their own families, some time around the year A.D. 2000.

THE SMALL-FAMILY NORM: SOCIOLOGICAL CONSIDERATIONS

The realization of any level of fertility, within certain physiologically determined upper limits, is dependent upon the strength of certain social pressures and conscious desires and is unrelated to the availability or efficiency of modern contraceptive technology.

There is abundant evidence from studies of traditional societies and pre-industrial Europe, for example, to indicate that in the complete absence of modern means of contraception, when social goals can best be met through a reduction in fertility, then that decrease is necessarily achieved (see discussions in Freeman 1970 and Geoffrey Hawthorn 1970a). Thus the rise in modern contraceptive technology can be viewed as a *response* to a demand for more acceptable and effective means of realizing the desired goal of lower fertility, and not (as is frequently advocated) as a *cause* of the observed reduction in fertility. For that important reason, the present discussion of population issues in Canada will explicitly avoid consideration of birth-control techniques, but will seek to outline more especially the social determinants of fertility.

Earlier it was stated that there is apparent in Canada a secular trend resulting in smaller family size. The current decline is 0.0275 children per year; thus, at the present rate, about twenty years are required to effect a reduction in completed family size from 3.5 to 3.0 children.

What are the social factors causing this trend? Presumably, if these elements could be identified, then social policy could be formulated which would enable governments to alter the rate and extent of population growth. In theory this manipulation of national population growth is quite possible, and the success of a few such government programs, especially in Japan and certain Eastern European countries, in managing demographic and economic reconstruction bears witness to this fact. It is as well to remember, however, that the incentive and/or necessity to make adaptive changes of this nature in one society may not appear as compelling in another, and so the specifics of the "success stories" are not so relevant for our present purpose as the generalizations to be derived from comparative studies in history and sociology pertaining to changed fertility levels.

It is pertinent to observe that the secular trend resulting in smaller completed-family size has been underway in Canada for some decades now despite an absence of any explicit policy favouring lowered fertility. On the other hand, many national policies relating to, for example, immigration, taxation, and social assistance benefits—by design (as with immigration) or inadvertently (as in certain fiscal arrangements)—either promote fertility or at least do nothing to discourage the maintenance of prevailing high fertility rates. As is well known, the implicit pro-natalistic thinking of our political and economic leaders has kept in force outmoded statutes that interfere with the goal of lower fertility (see, for example, McTaggart Cowan 1969, and Keenleyside 1969) and in all regions of Canada today many individuals still cannot obtain cooperation from local hospital or medical authorities in their legal and constitutional efforts to rationally control their individual fertility. Despite the persistence of such reactionary institutional tendencies, however, and in accord with the axiom stated earlier, levels of fertility *will* nonetheless change in the direction of people's perceived best interest; roadblocks thrown in the path may affect the speed with which society attains that goal, but even outright prohibitions will not prevent its ultimate achievement.

An important pioneering study on the comparative sociology of fertility has identified eleven intervening variables which can affect the fertility of a given population by means of the weight accorded each item. Thus, for example, pre-industrial societies in general place high value on such variables as a high rate of marriage and an early age of entering marriage compared with a generally lower value placed on these same fertility-promoting factors by industrial societies. On the other hand, pre-industrial societies place correspondingly high value on such fertility-lowering behaviour as, for example, ritually prescribed restrictions on sexual intercourse, or abortion, or on widow marriage. The conclusion was reached that, despite there being some effect exerted by *each* of the eleven variables, normative low fertility among industrial populations is not the result of low-fertility promoting value being placed on *all* the intermediate variables, but rather by the selection of *certain* variables, whose emphasis becomes the means to attain the goal of lowered fertility. It is apparent too that the means selected invokes both the least institutional re-organization and the least human cost (Davis and Blake 1956). This latter conclusion is particularly important to keep in mind when proposing policies designed to persuade people to alter their fertility norms.

There have been a number of institutional changes taking place in Canadian society, as part of the historical process of modernization, and it is within the context of these alterations that we should seek the cause of the secular trend of lowered fertility. The major population shift, from a rural-agricultural to an urban-industrial setting, has been noted earlier; it is commonly observed that this near-universal shift during modernization brings with it a corresponding reduction in fertility. The reasons for this are necessarily complex, and will involve, among other factors, a perception of decreasing "value" and increasing "cost" of children, rising levels of education both achieved and possible within the modern/urban setting, growing participation of women in a wage-earning economy, a shift in involvement from small, family-based, social and economic relationships toward involvement with larger, impersonal, institutional affinities, and an increased secularization of attitudes resulting in a lessened influence of these earlier-held opinions traditionally favouring high fertility. The complex interrelationships among these (and other) factors can be summed up by saying that there are, in the new setting, increasing opportunity costs involved in child-rearing and, coupled with the newfound realities and aspirations generated by urban living, the net result is a change in reproductive behaviour eventually resulting in smaller families.

I have qualified the conclusion with the word "eventually," because in many regions an immediate effect of the urbanization/modernization complex is a dramatic decrease in mortality, more especially in child mortality, so that larger rather than smaller families are often a consequence. In Canada where rural health standards have, for the most part, been sufficiently organized to reduce high mortality rates (though see, for example, Thomas 1968, and Musson 1971, for the situation among Canadian Indians and Eskimos), urbanization more quickly leads to an overall drop in numbers of children. This decrease is presumably dependent, however, upon a sufficient degree of involvement of urban residents with a lifestyle based on higher aspirations, one that offers hope and promise of social and economic advancement for oneself and one's children. Where no such favourable prognosis exists, there is little likelihood that fertility rates will decrease in mere response to relocation in urban centres.

THE SMALL-FAMILY NORM: ECONOMIC CONSIDERATIONS

Demographers and historians have long observed that economic variables and levels of fertility are related one to the other in an important manner. This affinity appears to hold through time, both within and between cultures, so that either the economic advance of a nation or the between-generation, shifting economic status of parents and their children have been used as an explanatory model to account for changing levels of fertility. Such events as the post-war "baby-booms" are frequently interpreted by reference to expanding economic opportunities, and the economic miracle of post-war Japan has been explained by reference to the dramatic decline of that country's birth-rate. Recent reviews have comprehensively explored the connection between socio-economic status and reproductive behaviour (for example, Freedman and Coombs 1966, Easterlin 1969). Suffice it to say here that there is a complex interrelationship between various positive and negative economic values, so that a solution to a very difficult, and perhaps insoluble, cost-benefit equation is necessary before a rational decision can be made as to whether the cost of adding a child to a household outweighs the benefit. It goes without saying that "cost" and "benefit" certainly involve a great many non-economic and non-objective values. For this latter reason, especially, the analytic tools of the economist, rather than the substantive data he works with, may represent the greatest single contribution the science of economics can make to our understanding of reproductive behaviour (see, for example, the theoretical discussions by the noted demographer and economist Dr. Joseph J. Spengler, 1966).

A model, familiar to economic analysts, has been suggested to explain the changing value accorded children in a society experiencing increasing economic opportunities; an adaptation of this model is presented as Figure 1 (see Leibenstein 1957 for the original formulation).

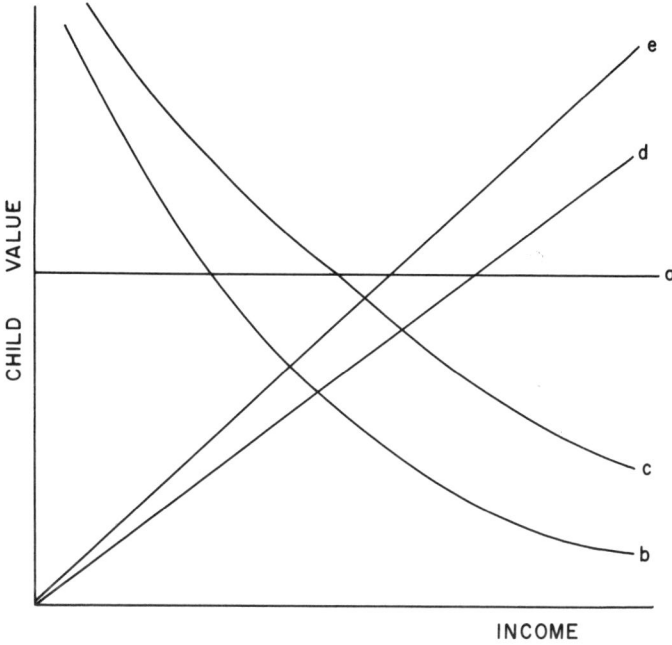

FIGURE 1. Model illustrating changing utility value of children in relation to shifting economic opportunities.

Horizontal line (a) indicates that the intrinsic value of a child remains unchanged in relation to changing levels of income; this is the one main assumption entered in this model, though the concession is made that the level it attains on the vertical axis may well be different according to the sex or birth-order of the individual infant. On the other hand, the value of a child as a contributor to the income (b) declines as economic status of the society (or family) increases, as does the value afforded the child as a provider of security in the parents' old age (c). There are, in addition to these decreasing utility values, a series of increasing costs incurred by children as parental income rises: higher revenue causes a direct demand as more costly child-rearing accoutrements (d) are deemed necessary (for example, costs of education, material items, cultural activities) and rising indirect opportunity costs (e) (for example, provision of a higher quality environment for children causes certain economic options, otherwise open to the parents, to be foregone). It is the sum of the increasing direct and indirect costs (d + e) together with the decrease in utility added $-(b + c)$ that *in toto* cause thresholds in perceived value to be crossed, thus precipitating re-evaluation of the rational bases of normative (high) fertility.

Where income is high, but great value continues to be placed on children (a), then the decision reached may well be to postpone having children rather than either invoke high opportunity costs at that time or decide in favour of a smaller family size. It is apparent in recently modernized societies, or those still undergoing modernization, that incomes tend to rise at a faster rate than values change in respect to high fertility; it often happens that opportunity costs (d + e) do not outweigh the aggregate positive value $(a_1 + a_2 + a_3 \ldots \ldots + a_n)$ for children, until after "n" children have been added to the family. It is in these societies that family-planning programs fall far short of the means or goals normally set by explicit population policies. This is the situation pertaining in certain mostly non-urbanized, though incipiently modernized, regions of Canada (for example, the Atlantic Provinces) where family-planning programs are unlikely by themselves to effectively accelerate the rate of fertility decline.

THE SMALL-FAMILY NORM: MOTIVATIONAL ASPECTS

Sociological explanations, to be useful for purposes of formulating social policy, must necessarily deal with less tangible and visible information than that merely derived through empirical observations. Thus to observe that an excellent correlation exists between, for example, working wives and small family size is neither intellectually very satisfying nor heuristically very useful. Only when the role of a number of important intervening variables is understood will the true meaning and full implication of that first level of generalization be uncovered. It may be that working wives have, on the average, more education that non-working wives (so is it educational level attained or wage employment which depresses fertility?), or that working wives are married to men holding different attitudes towards women's role in society, or that working wives include a high proportion of those women who are materially acquisitive and who consequently view children as costly alternate items of consumption. Certainly such a list of plausible intervening factors suggests that what women *think* about certain goals, roles, or alternate choices is of crucial importance if one wishes a full understanding of their reproductive behaviour.

Most people, and especially women, recognize a psychological as well as a social and physical need for marriage and parenthood. These felt needs, however, are perceived in response to cultural as well as biological imperatives. The reason for the culturally conditioned imperative is that reproduction and socialization of offspring are not intrinsically important tasks for the individual, *except* insofar as that individual is a member of a social group sharing a common set of values favouring that group's continued existence through time. Thus, traditionally, high value has been placed on reproduction, *by the group,* through the dictates of its culture. The norms are necessarily in the direction of high, rather than low, fertility because, in the face of high risks of mortality prevailing prior to the advent of modern medicine, only repeated child-bearing could ensure that each pair of parents would replace itself by at least one child of each sex reaching reproductive age—a necessity if a small group is to perpetuate itself. Furthermore, because people sometimes tend to be selfish, and might, for example, choose the life of a carefree bachelor over assumption of family responsibility, cultural norms also created and fostered an acute perception of individual need for producing children. This need might be created by the requirement to have a son survive his parent's death, so that the son could conduct certain important ritual observances to ensure the welfare of the parent after death. Beliefs such as these have often made it very difficult to introduce the small-family ideal into traditional, pre-modern societies until such time as mortality rates have been demonstrably lowered, so that people can convince themselves that repeated child-bearing is no longer necessary to ensure their being survived by at least one son.

It is unlikely, given the changed attitudes to death rituals and the altered institutional setting in which old age occurs (the availability of pensions, retirement homes, and the like), that child-bearing in Canada or other similarly modernized societies is viewed in these traditionally important ways. The immediate or short-term rewards or sanctions connected with a particular activity are likely to have considerably greater import, for it is generally held by sociologists that behaviour will probably be repeated (and hence eventually become normative), depending to a great extent on the degree to which that behaviour is consistently and continually rewarded. Positive sanctions (rewards) tend to be more effective in influencing behaviour than are negative sanctions (penalties), for it appears likely that people come to believe they can always outsmart the system, a belief that seriously detracts from the threat posed by the stick, but which does nothing to disparage the appeal of the carrot.

The non-reward, though not actually a negative sanction, can be so construed by a society which normatively seeks to maximize gain for purposes of encouraging adaptive changes in customary behaviour and attitudes. Therefore, society might be well advised not merely to penalize certain antisocial or otherwise undesirable behaviours but rather to explicitly reward conformity to new adaptive norms considered desirable.

A PROBLEM WITH PREDICTION

In attempting to show an inverse relationship between economic status and fertility I have necessarily overgeneralized almost to the point of compromising the canons of science (for a comprehensive analysis of intervening variables affecting fertility, see Geoffrey Hawthorn 1970a).

Even now, some inconsistencies in the data presented might be apparent: for example, was not the post-war "baby-boom" occurring during a period of *increasing* prosperity? Furthermore, the latest census figures from Britain and the United States indicate that fertility among the higher socio-economic groups, rather than continuing to decline, appears to be on the increase.

There are a variety of possible explanations to account for these observations. It could be hypothesized that in economically secure families there is less motivation for perfect contraceptive behaviour, for in these families an unplanned pregnancy will not be so damaging to family well-being. Equally plausible is the hypothesis that wives of highly paid executives or professional men are less likely to work and so probably seek fulfilment by having a larger family. Or that children, being an expensive commodity, have become something of a status symbol in their own right among families already owning a mansion, two cars, a cottage, a boat, colour TV, and every labour-saving gadget on the market.

The sociological literature does not, at this time, allow for satisfactory answers to the question: Why the apparent upswing in fertility among the higher socio-economic strata of modern society? There is, however, an important cautionary aspect to be deduced from this empirical observation.

Often in explaining social behaviour it is necessary to remain aware that a time lag operates, because of the later manifestation of earlier socializing pressures. Thus, for example, to return to the "baby-boom" phenomenon, it would be possible, in relation to the utility model presented earlier (page 123), to account for the greater fertility of post-war marriages by saying that the greater economic opportunities and future prospects encouraged people to produce children with more abandon. This implies however that those couples' *tastes* (or needs?) for children were stronger than their tastes (or needs) for the various consumer items similarly competing for their economic wherewithal. It has been suggested that we can understand the post-war generation's reproductive behaviour by remembering that these people were socialized in childhood during a period of relative economic stringency, and also that they fell heir to a necessarily enforced low value on consumerism during several years of wartime shortages (Easterlin 1966).

Can we use this line of reasoning to cautiously forecast future fertility trends in Western industrial societies, including Canada? It seems likely that many intervening variables will be acting to lower fertility: higher rates of unemployment and under-employment engendering feelings of uncertain future economic prospects, greater access to and prevalence of more effective contraception, childhood socialization having occurred during a time of greater affluence and thus causing a continuing high value to be placed on consumerism, a probably greater participation of women in the labour force (due to prevailing women's lib ideology as well as economic pressures on newlyweds), to mention but a few.

Yet, given the availability of contraception and the economic prospects, one of the most potent means of lowering fertility, namely, by delaying entry into marriage, is unlikely to be widespread, for when wives go out to work two can most assuredly live, if not cheaper, then certainly better than one. The crucial factor then, having created a social setting (by entry into marriage) at least partially conducive to reproduction, is whether social pressures will be exerted on young married couples to "start a family." At this point we must remember, too, the time-lag effect: the fact that today's young adults were socialized at a time when the prevailing ideology was to have children at a young enough age to enjoy them, and to be actively engaged with them in "having fun" whilst growing up. Of course ideologies change; indeed, if they did not there would be little point in education. With regard to education, however, it does not necessarily follow that influences from that quarter are adaptive; we are reminded:

> For many years . . . Dick and Jane dominated the six year old scene. In the first grade readers there was Mother and Daddy—and Dick and Jane. Two children at least; never less. If there was a married couple next door they had children too. The people across the street had children. Everyone worth mentioning—everybody who *was* mentioned—had children. . . . The childish mind was filled with only one picture of the Good Life: to be married and have children. (Hardin 1969b: 312–3.)

There is a strong tendency to continue, perhaps unconsciously, the perpetuation of such time-honoured stereotypes. The point to remember, if we are to effect the orderly demographic adaptation Professor Blake calls for, is that attention needs to be given to all such matters, for adult role-playing obtains powerful sanction from the imprinting that occurs during early childhood and the so-called formative years.

THE LIMITS OF GOVERNMENTAL INTERCESSION

The question whether governments have the "right" (in a

democratic state) to interfere with individuals' hitherto almost unlimited freedom to breed depends upon several important considerations. These will include, among other things: the degree to which compulsion or coercion rather than persuasion, or free choice between alternatives, is employed; the exact nature of the "right" that people believe they are relinquishing; and their perception of the implications of that particular surrender (for instance: "if government takes over and decides on birth, they will take over death control next!"). Because the adverse effect people may exert on the environment is primarily related to what those people do, and only secondarily to their numbers or spatial distribution, many of the environmental problems exacerbated by population size, density, distribution, or growth could be overcome by measures other than controlling fertility. For example: a massive relocation of people, out of the burgeoning metropolitan areas, back to the rural areas where model communities of optimum size (perhaps 100,000 to 250,000?) might be built; a more selective immigration policy; closing down of pollution-intensive industries (such as paper mills, steel mills, some mining and smelting operations, chemical industries) unless they were to clean up their operations completely; restricting all but pollution-free transportation systems; a reduction in electricity consumption; and a reduction in ecologically destructive agricultural practices. The list could go on, but this Orwellian spectre, entailing control and inspection, suggesting an even greater governmental involvement in our daily affairs, and our access to fewer of the good things in life, is surely unacceptable to the reader. The time has come, however, when certain considered choices do have to be made, for doing nothing (or too little) *is* doing something (by default), namely, exerting an increasingly powerful strain upon the environment, which in turn further reduces the choices available for corrective action in the future.

Many years ago, the Scottish physician Sir Dugal Baird referred to a fifth basic freedom, namely, the "freedom from the tyranny of excessive fertility"; he was speaking of the incubus of excess fertility at the family or individual level, though even then the cost, in terms of human degradation and wastage, was borne by all society. Today, however, the investment that society is called upon to make for each birth occurring is considerably greater; the annual cost to the state is, in approximate direct financial terms, calculated to be about one and one-half times the annual average per capita income, or about $5000 per child per year in Canada. Parenthetically I might reiterate that there is no economic gain to developed nations from an increase in population size, though a slower rate of population growth is economically beneficial in the developed nations just as in the less-developed (Westoff and Westoff 1968: 342).

But our focus here is not economic but ecologic: in regard to that perspective, a leading environmentalist has suggested that: "a creative pause in procreation—a non-proliferation pact with ourselves—may be the best hope for the next decade" (Udall 1970: 7).

The question remains unanswered, however: namely, how justifiable is it, for government or for any group in society, to decide that a restriction must be imposed on individual fertility?

Government has the duty to govern, and part of that governance must be concerned with future states as well as the present. Indeed, the daily business of administration requires continual encroachment upon present-day privileges, "rights," and amenities to adequately safeguard the nation's future health. We accept the following actions as not only necessary but responsible acts of government: compulsory pension and other welfare deductions, expropriation of land for urban land banks, national parks, and communication facilities, compulsory schooling, immunization, incarceration. More than a decade ago, scientist and man of letters, C. P. Snow wrote (1961): "All healthy societies are ready to sacrifice the existential moment for their children's future and for children after these. The sense of the future is behind all good policies. Unless we have it, we can give nothing either wise or decent to the world."

Some writers (for example, Berman 1970, Chasteen 1972) believe that voluntary efforts are too slow-acting to produce the necessary non-proliferation of people, and that a political responsibility exists which cannot long be ignored by responsible leaders of all nations. In the United States as an example, population programs received an allotment of less than a half-million dollars in 1964, an amount which had increased fortyfold by 1970. Times and circumstances do change, and some leaders have the courage to move things along. In 1959 then-President Eisenhower stated: "I cannot imagine anything more emphatically a subject that is not a proper political or government activity . . . this government will not . . . as long as I am here, have a positive political doctrine in its program that has to do with this problem of birth control. That's not our business." In 1968 Eisenhower admitted: "Once, as President, I thought and said that birth control was not the business of our Federal Government. The facts have changed my mind . . . I have come to believe that the population explosion is the world's most critical problem."

At the time that Eisenhower publicly announced his change of mind, the Canadian Parliament was debating a section of the Criminal Code that prohibited dissemination of information on birth control and sale of contraceptives in Canada; a reversal was not effected until 1969. But the proscriptions of the law ("the imbecile prohibition that has stained our Criminal Code," according to a distinguished Canadian, Hugh Keenleyside, in 1968) were mostly ignored at home, so much so and with such inequity as to compromise the cause of social justice in this country. Indeed, the social injustices resulting from this largely unenforced and anachronistic proscription moved the Catholic bishops of Canada to present to the Commons Committee on Health and Welfare a brief calling for repeal of the law, aiming toward legalizing birth control in Canada. The international implications of Canadian inability at home to regard birth control as legal, and therefore proper, has been summarized elsewhere (Keenleyside 1969), and points to the necessity of frank discussion of population issues. As this book attempts to show, the interrelationships between events at home and abroad are so intimately forged, the nature of the population-related problems so fundamentally similar, that for any nation to attempt to chart a narrowly national route to ecological salvation is both logically unsound and practically unworkable.

With respect to population policy formulation, we might start by observing that, as mentioned earlier, the role of government in promoting the national welfare of all its citizens has long been accepted. In those countries where governments either have instituted population policies or are involved in national family-planning programs, the justification for this action is sought in terms of extending the freedom of choice of citizens or of otherwise enhancing human welfare. Since both of these are considered legitimate concerns of governments, and since demographic trends can very significantly affect these objectives, it appears within the right of national administrations to adopt policies and to implement or facilitate programs aimed at serving these two ends.

There exists a long historic precedent for government intervention in the fields of procreation-related behaviour: specifically pronatalistic population policies have influenced procreation in a positive fashion and the legal regulation of marriage and sexual encounters has also directly and indirectly controlled fertility. It would seem, therefore, that government in the past has been allowed to intervene in this area of human behaviour to the same degree as in other areas where individual and collective welfare appears to be at issue.

If forms of intervention specifically antinatalistic in nature are now called for, it does not appear that any new ethical or political principle is being invoked or challenged. Indeed, this extension of government action confirms the classical argument for the need of government, namely, that some formal and public mechanism is required to regulate the exercise of individual liberty for the common good. Indeed, we expect that our administration will take the steps necessary to ensure and promote the common good, and if the measures proposed are at first unpalatable then good government requires that educational programs be instigated to enlighten the population as to why such policies and programs are considered necessary. The duty of good government is, explicitly, to act in the interests of the population, to observe and respect citizens' rights, to respect national values, and to guarantee justice and equality. Since population growth among other factors can, and does, affect all of these aspects of national life, positive and effective response to the challenge of population-induced change is clearly and uncontestably within the area of government responsibility.

Faced with a population problem that has to do, among other things, with the question of growth, a national government has several options open; it can (1) do nothing; (2) expand activity in the field of voluntarism (that is, expand family planning and related educational information programs); (3) institute programs that go beyond family planning (that is, involving involuntary or coercive means of reducing fertility).

Under (3), some have advocated a stepwise progression involving systems of licensing (every couple entitled to produce two children, and more if they can purchase someone's unused licence), or heavy sanctions to encourage low fertility or to discourage higher levels of fertility, tampering with the national diet or water supply, compulsory sterilization of those nonconforming to national fertility norms (see, for example, Berelson's 1969 important review). Although most people will opt for alternative (2), that is, an expansion of purely voluntary programs, it should be remembered that both morally and practically a very thin (and movable) line separates options (2) and (3) under certain circumstances. For example, if incentives are employed to motivate people to avail themselves of voluntary programs, at what point does taking, or refusing, a material incentive cease to be a matter of free choice? It is perfectly conceivable that need (in a materially deprived person) might have "forced" that person to accept an inducement thereby availing himself coincidentally of the program the incentive aims to encourage. This inadvertent and unintended restriction of choice becomes even more likely where a truly effective system of incentives is designed in an especial effort to keep the population program on a voluntary basis. This therefore becomes one strong moral reason for starting population programs earlier rather than later, for voluntarism may all too soon become an unretainable luxury in a society where social equality and justice are prime values to be preserved at any cost (for an example of a fertility-control program which aims to be socially equitable even though involuntary, the reader is referred to Ketchel 1968). Unfortunately then, voluntary programs, though ostensibly retaining the basic freedom of choice we claim as an important value, do so unequally and are consequently likely to preserve the rights of the majority at the expense of the minority. (Judith Blake makes this same point in questioning the utility of family-planning programs aimed at particular segments of society; see Blake 1969.) As such, the ethical basis of this type of program is severely undermined unless we subscribe to the position that moral good, and hence justification, is served by electing to effect the greatest good for the greatest number, or that the principle of choosing between the lesser of two evils is a morally just course of action to follow.

To some extent the moral dilemmas entered above can be overcome by making incentives of such a nature that in addition to averting births they also confer other social benefits. An example would be a cash bond redeemable at the normal time of retirement, thus ensuring a level of security and comfort that might otherwise have ultimately become available to the parents had they earlier produced an additional (now financially established) child. Such bonds would serve the added useful function of income redistribution, which, incidentally, was the original purpose of the family-allowance system.

Some writers have proposed various negative incentives; for example, punitively high levels of taxation in families of more than two children, or withdrawal of welfare benefits or free education or health insurance in the event of families increasing beyond a certain permissible size. Such schemes should be rejected as ethically unacceptable, for they compromise the important social value of distributive justice insofar as the penalties would be felt to a greater extent by already poor families, whereas the rich transgressor might incur the penalty with relative impunity. Such sanctions similarly compromise the principle of freedom of choice, as they effectively deny that freedom to poor families although permitting the more economically secure families to exercise that choice. Added to these powerful reasons for rejecting negative sanctions is the important one that such a policy would seriously prejudice the ideal of manifold social benefit accruing from the population policy (which must be the main goal of such a policy), for the decrees would effectively withhold a worthwhile financial supplement or subsidy to those families most in need of such additional income support.

We might also note that penalty schemes, to be effective, would probably require an enforcement system that would by its very nature lead to a reduction in the quality of life that the population policy itself is seeking to enhance. The question must be faced, however: does not a government have a right, if not a moral responsibility, at some point to restrict the freedom of choice of its citizens for the sake of future generations? This is a difficult question to resolve, for we can argue logically, in legal and moral terms, about the rights of people alive but not so unequivocably about people who do not yet exist (even if we know they will exist). The answer might be that until we have tried, honestly and energetically (which we have not yet done), to make non-coercive programs work, it might appear both arbitrary and unwarranted to set aside the rights of the living for the potential rights of the not-yet living. Others have pointed out that making decisions and setting standards for future generations is a rather presumptuous, if not irrational, exercise; however, we clearly do have an obligation to leave a physically inhabitable environment to posterity, even if our aesthetic standards and social arrangements are unlikely to be those that future generations will wish to share or bother to preserve. In summary then, there does seem to be a present-day individual and collective duty to conserve rather than waste, to set aside rather than despoil, and to generally limit those of our activities which would tend to contribute to a situation which we, in our wisdom, are unable to correct (even if the impact of such activities will only be fully manifest at some undetermined time in the future).

The conclusion must be then that government has a clear and compelling immediate duty to become involved in expanding those voluntary programs that will most likely effect a significant and sustained reduction in population growth and thereby obviate the need for precipitate adoption of programs of a coercive and restrictive nature at a future date.

For a fuller treatment of ethical and practical problems surrounding government involvements in population-limiting policies, the reader is referred to Berelson (1969) and Callahan (1972), whose excellent studies strongly influence the views expressed above.

Chapter Seven

FUTURE DIRECTIONS: RATIONALIZING THE ISSUE

The problems facing mankind as a collectivity certainly have no technical solution when viewed from the standpoint of the individual. Just as the spectre of overpopulation threatens us all, not only as members of the human species but as an integral part of the beleaguered biosphere, so the solution must be one which extends the basis of our rational thinking, indeed our morality, to encompass all co-tenants of planet Earth. As philosopher Abraham Edel reminds us in an article in *Transaction* (January 1972), "Morality is self-making and society-making and there is no cut between the two."

Given the pending if not present necessity of a new universal ethic, the impertinence and amorality of sectional interests serving to block progress toward this realization should be readily apparent. This reactionary caucus includes such establishment giants as certain large international corporations (whose mindless growth demands continual creation of needless wants), national governments (that continue to test atomic devices, for example), and the Roman Catholic Church (which continues to implicitly condone overpopulation by condemning certain voluntary and effective means of fertility control). With respect to the latter, though no significant numbers privately obey Catholic teaching on birth control, those pronouncements nevertheless somehow serve effectively to slow public adoption of certain rational means of treating human overproduction. One could argue that if man *were* truly a rational being, he would first condemn, then quickly disregard, any teaching that promotes injustice, hypocrisy, and human, physical, and spiritual suffering (for examples, see the article on family planning in Eire: O'Donnell 1970). Although no one would deny the piety and sincerity of Catholic belief, the irrational and unwarranted basis of that belief for non-Catholics nevertheless remains (see, for example, Minority Report, Papal Study Commission 1966, reported in Stanford 1972: 214; also H. L. Smith 1971: 213, McLennan 1972: 5–6).

Notwithstanding the views of a right-wing minority, for the majority of people today the earlier certitude of religious teaching in most matters now has less saliency because of the host of new, complex, and essentially man-made problems that burst upon the global scene each year. It is extremely foolish, however, to replace an earlier blind faith in theological pronouncement with an equally blind faith in the power of science and technology to provide answers to questions posed by the current dilemmas of human existence. The temptation certainly exists to seek answers in areas of strength, and putting men into space and bringing them home again is proof enough for some that all problems are, eventually, scientifically soluble. Moreover, the value of science to our current situation is that it gives us a means of approaching problems, though it in no way guarantees us correct answers to these issues. Science *might* work, it might solve the problems, *if* we had all the correct data necessary to attain complete understanding and *if* we then acted according to the instructions on the computer print-out—in other words, if we would wish to make science our master rather than our servant, expending most of our disposable income on support of expensive research projects and then doing as the electronic brains demanded. This of course implies such a complete surrender of our humanness as to be totally unacceptable.

What if we were to just behave rationally, where "rational" means that, given a free choice between two alternatives, individuals will exercise that option and select the alternative offering the greater utility. Unfortunately, even postulating this ideal state of complete rationality will not ensure that wrong decisions will not be made (for both simple and complex examples, see Wallace 1972: 250–56). Ecologist Paul B. Sears has stated this very well in his classic book, *Deserts on the March* (1935): "Science has the power to illuminate, but not to solve the deeper problems of mankind. For always after knowledge comes choice and action, both of them intensely personal and individual. . . . But we must bear in mind that science as such, affords us no sanction. It may inform us with regard to any social or economic system but it cannot make decisions for us." The point to be remembered is that even though decision-making procedures may be correct, the options arrived at can, nevertheless, be bad ones (for example, tactical errors in warfare, or fiscal policies aimed at curbing inflation which increase unemployment to socially disruptive levels). The moral plainly is that decisions taken where error may lead to serious or irreparable damage must be made by extraordinarily thoughtful, not routine, procedures.

Unfortunately, the time has come, or is imminent perhaps, when we will no longer be able to make routine pronouncements about solving our earthly environment-related problems. As stressed earlier, I am not forecasting our imminent physical demise as a species, for I believe the issue to be centred on the nature and manner of our future existence rather than the question of ensuring mere survival. We need to take stock of our situation with objectivity and openness, and I would add fearlessness, too, for the implications of moving away from time-honoured ideology and comforting conformity will be a challenging and awesome adventure for the majority of us. But we desperately need a new morality, an ethical system which will not impede, as our present ones appear to do, but rather will facilitate exercise of our rational capabilities in pursuit of greater human well-being. This rethinking of our values will necessitate questioning the very basis of our social, political, and economic systems; yet such a catharsis may itself be rewarding, for in another social or economic situation the present population-precipitated problems may appear less intractable and thereby involve fewer conflict-promoting ideological confrontations. If, on the other hand, we steadfastly refuse even to consider changes to the existing institutional order, then we are trapped into seeking needed solutions in terms that are limited by the very systemic dysfunctions that have precipitated the problems we now desperately must solve.

Primarily, I see the need in this nation for a humane population policy whose goal is an overall increase in social welfare; such a platform will be more acceptable the more its goals serve a broad range of other socially beneficial objectives. A population policy, then, has a potential for coincidentally effecting long-overdue reforms in a host of cognate and deserving areas of national and international life. A brief to the Federal Commission on Population Growth and the American Future cogently phrased such sentiments thus: "A population policy should attempt to serve freedom, justice, the general welfare and security/survival by *pushing forward* the frontiers and implementation of those values . . . it will not be enough to be satisfied with the mere preservation of these values as they now exist. For the way in which they now exist is *defective,* in many instances a genuine scandal" (Anon. 1971: 2).

Though these views were written about the United States, they apply with equal force to Canada and to certain other nations too. As Professor F. H. Knelman of Sir George Williams University in Montreal has written, this is the age of Big Government, wherein complex bureaucracies with heavy techno-scientific and big-business involvement move nations to destiny or destruction. According to Professor Knelman, decision-making, and hence rationality itself, is in this context largely illusory, for "the System," now a blind juggernaut primed for self-perpetuation and growth, has taken control even though locked onto a collision course with cataclysm.

The great need of the times appears to be for an operational ethic, a new morality, which will work toward the creation of real social justice nationally and, by logical and automatic extension, internationally also. Utopian, you say? Only if I were to assert or plead that such a desirable state of affairs be achieved or initiated overnight or nearly so. I certainly do not proclaim such an unrealizable objective, nor do I envisage a near-complete or rapid revision of all human values and attitudes. Although I realize *piecemeal* "solutions" to our problems will achieve nothing substantial, I nevertheless believe that, given the complexity of the problems, a realistic course of action must be programmed in such a way as to initiate a stepwise (though integrative) orderly succession of reforms. The vision of this particular mortal being strictly limited, I can only see as far as the first, though perhaps most important, step in this progression, namely, toward a national population-policy commission, a *permanent* institution reporting regularly to the nation concerning the implications of current demographic behaviour for the whole field of national welfare.

Specifically, such a commission should be reporting on its evaluation of the various social, economic, and political consequences of projected population changes, and advising on the actions needed to promote those consequences considered desirable, and to prevent those considered undesirable. Although in some countries, like the United States and Britain, population commissions are attached to the office of the president or prime minister, that arrangement might be less than desirable because of the intensely political nature of such an office; complete separation (as with the Privy Council, or the Economic or Science Councils of Canada) is clearly preferable for a body which must look critically at the nation's health and at the policies and leaders responsible for that condition.

PRIORITIES

Having stated that an immediate goal should be the development of a national population policy, let me now outline certain consequences of seeking such an objective. This section is headed "priorities" but there can be no simple or straightforward ordering of events, for, given the urgency and complexity of the task, all matters relating to the formulation of such a policy must be seen as deserving equal and pressing attention. Unfortunately, there is a great deal that needs to be understood about the Canadian population process, in terms not only of research and training but also of the political and ethical viability of any such reforms as may be considered necessary and desirable.

One example of an issue requiring more information and social evaluation is abortion. This is one topic that generates discussion from a variety of perspectives and upon which few people hold no view whatsoever. I suggest that we focus momentarily on abortion for a number of pertinent reasons: because it directs our attention to an ethical issue based on a widely diverging spectrum of historical and contemporary ideological viewpoints (which ultimately will require resolution); because no country has ever controlled its population growth without recourse to abortion; because it is the commonest form of birth control in the world today (and in the past); because the demand for abortion in modern society will probably increase rather than decline; because many new chemical (and mechanical) birth-control techniques rely in part on abortion-producing action; and because abortion, a topic long tabooed, is shrouded by information of questionable validity as well as suffering from an absence of much pertinent information.

The last point is worth taking first, by way of example. Many of our current ideas about abortion are the result of historically important views, which should be understood in evaluating the saliency of these opinions in modern terms. For example, abortion was once a dangerous, and therefore proscribed exercise, so hazardous a medical procedure in the days before anaesthetics (1846) and antiseptics (1867) that it almost invariably resulted in the death, or seriously impaired function, of the mother. Thus, in 1809 it was classed in British law as murder (unless to save the life of the mother), and plainly discouraged under penalty of death. It was unlawful, not only because of the serious medical consequences, but also because the only people willing to undertake the act were either non-licensed lay people or unethical medical practitioners—unethical because abortion contravened the 2000–year-old Hippocratic oath taken by doctors of that day—and both classes of person would thereby be categorized as felons. Death was a common penalty paid by convicted felons of the nineteenth century. The law was promulgated for practical medical and civil, rather than moral, reasons.

Today a number of significant changes have occurred. Firstly, few medical schools require allegiance to an unmodified Hippocratic oath, a reform clearly made necessary by advances in modern medicine (McLachlan 1971, Reid 1972, Veatch 1972). Abortion is no longer a particularly dangerous or hazardous surgical practice; in fact it has become an outpatient, or doctor's office, procedure under optimal conditions (of early pregnancy), and in some countries is carried out by para-medical personnel. Indeed, the risks of dying in childbirth are many times greater in Canada (at 27/100,000) than are those of dying from the consequences of abortion in several European countries (for example, 1.0/100,000 abortions in Czechoslovakia; 2.2/100,000 in Hungary) or in the United States (8.2/100,000).

While on the subject of medicine, we may take the medical profession to illustrate the wide range of opinions with respect to abortion existing today within different sectors of Canadian society. Thus, whereas the British Columbia College of Physicians in 1971 reinstated a doctor who had earlier been fined $15,000 and jailed for performing 1000 illegal abortions, in 1972 full-page advertisements were placed in three provincial newspapers by a group of forty-one Newfoundland doctors who whole-heartedly condemned the practice of abortion.

Some of the differences between opinions could be reduced by greater exposure of the topic to informed discussion (see, for example, Lader 1966). As an illustration of misinformation clouding the issue, it is widely believed that permitting abortion will open the door to a host of other forms of homicide—such as senilicide, euthanasia—on specious, indeed trivial, and thinly disguised pretexts. Despite the fact that such has not occurred (and indeed is unlikely to occur, see Wallace 1972: 83–86) in any modern society allowing voluntary abortion, the belief nevertheless persists without factual basis in North America today. Others claim pragmatic grounds for opposing an easing of abortion restrictions, namely, that there would never be enough hospital beds if curbs were not maintained. Apart from present-day administrative reasons for localized overcrowding (see Pelrine 1971: 36–43), the federal Department of Health and Welfare has ascertained that no such bed shortage would arise for the simple reason that a properly instituted abortion service would function as an outpatient procedure, obviating the need for hospital beds (information given in reply to a Parliamentary Question, 15 May 1972; see also Tietze and Lewit 1972: 104 for United States data).

There is no evidence to suggest that women will get pregnant wilfully so as to have abortions, nor that this procedure would supplant contraception as the normal means of birth control; the role of abortion is as a back-stop method of limitation, when contraception has failed, to prevent an unwanted or potentially damaging conception from continuing to term. If we recall that the objectives of a population policy must logically serve a variety of beneficial social causes to be truly effective, the illogic of perpetuating the social injustices of the present abortion set-up in Canada clearly becomes indefensible.

Unfortunately, no nation can proceed very far on the road to reducing its population fertility without eventual recourse to liberalizing laws respecting therapeutic abortion, for reasons already discussed (pp. 108-9). We have therefore come face to face with a high-priority need in the matter of formulation of a national population policy, namely, education and public information programs to explain rationally the basis of our presently held beliefs. If people understood these bases, then they could act in an informed manner either to retain or to replace those particular ideas; without that essential basis of factual knowledge there remains the potential to act in a biased and partial manner, resulting in less chance of reaching a workable *rapprochement* with others holding equally sincere but opposing convictions (for an example, see McLennan 1972).

Another area of high priority must be the training of professionals in a wide range of population-related disciplines, and also the exposure of professionals in other disciplines to factual information on population-related topics. Perhaps these two aspects of the training problem are of equal importance, for the effects and implications of population change affect us all, yet are poorly, if at all, represented in our formal educational curricula at any level. In Canada some of the most articulate and vociferous advocates of a population policy are the professional biologists, and more especially the zoologists; they are among the few whose training generally includes study of the principles and ecological consequences of population change, albeit with species other than man.

School teachers, nurses, social workers, doctors, and the clergy are those most often in contact with the mass of the public; yet they are among the groups who receive either insignificant or no factual information on human demography. This dearth of intelligence manifests itself in the general lack of political involvement and concern of these professions in Canada with questions pertaining to domestic population issues. Not that there is a total lack of awareness of the fact that "population problems" pose a serious threat to mankind, but the danger is rarely perceived to be more proximate than the Indian subcontinent or Latin America.

Specifically, the fields of fertility and contraception are poorly represented in professional training programs, even in the health and welfare fields. Schools of social work in Canada held a national workshop in 1972 to discuss inclusion of human fertility and sexuality in their professional training curricula, but the topic had been received with very little enthusiasm when first suggested to these teachers during 1971.

The February 1972 issue of the *Newsletter* of the Newfoundland Medical Association carried a guest editorial by a pediatrician who pleaded for endorsement by that province's doctors of a proposed provincial family-planning association. The often tragic socio-medical consequences of high parity or unwanted pregnancy, added to the near absence of genetic counselling, voluntary sterilization, or family-planning facilities in that province, attest to the failure of medical education, at least in the recent past, to prepare doctors for the realities of providing comprehensive health care in a society where fertility remains at the high level of a pre-industrial period. Thus, in a panel discussion sponsored by a Newfoundland nurses' association in 1971, no one challenged the views of a psychiatrist who opined that a local 13–year-old, grade 8, student who was pregnant might be better off to have her child and face the responsibility of motherhood (rather than seek abortion): "There would be no reason for her to miss very much school . . . . I bet there's many a nurse who almost have their babies on duty" (reported in the St. John's *Evening Telegram,* 10 February 1971).

In the Canadian north today, women are being prescribed oral contraceptives even though they are breast-feeding their babies, a practice contra-indicated for endocrinological reasons, thus suggesting a serious ignorance by doctors and nurses of the physiological potency of the hormonal compounds being used. Unfortunately, too, the oral preparations made routinely available in the north have high estrogen content (either 80 or 100 micrograms), despite the recommendation of the Special Advisory Committee on Oral Contraceptives, reporting to the federal Health Minister in October 1970, that because of the link with thrombo-embolism "whenever possible physicians should be advised to prescribe a preparation containing not more than 50 micrograms of estrogen." Elsewhere, I have detailed the extent of medical, political, and administrative naïvity with regard to fertility behaviour, its control, and its implications in the Northwest Territories of Canada (Freeman 1971a, 1971b). The situation described, however, is not restricted merely to that underdeveloped region of Canada, as my remarks on Nova Scotia and Newfoundland may serve to show.

LICENCE TO BREED: CONCLUDING CONSIDERATIONS

The biblical injunction to be fruitful and multiply might have exerted some positive influence on fertility in the past, but it is likely that sanctions against various methods of birth control have had a more pronounced demographic effect. Even the Roman Catholic Church, the one major branch of Christianity still opposing effective action against unwanted conception, bases its stand not on the premise that contraception is evil because God ordered believers to be fruitful, but because throughout centuries of Papal teaching contraception has been equated with homicide.

In effect, Christian (and hence Euro-American secular) views on procreation have largely been shaped by reaction to what early Church leaders perceived as dangerous social or ideological trends of the times. Catholic historian John T. Noonan (1965) has provided the best discussion of these events, and should be read for a full account. In summary, however, we may note that the connection between Adam's original sin and human sexuality was sufficiently evident to early churchmen to make sexual intercourse an unpleasant, or at least an ethically ambiguous, activity. Abstinence and virginity were therefore wholly desirable states and the early Christians' abhorrence of the carnal excesses of Roman society reinforced their considerable concern for producing better, rather than more, people. Thus a contemporary writer, St. Basil, contrasted man and animals by the observation that whereas animals grow by bodily and numerical increase, man multiplies by spiritual growth and rise in good works.

During the fourth century A.D., when Christianity became the official religion of the Roman Empire, a rival religion founded by the prophet Mani became popular. The Manicheans believed sexual activity was good, and therefore condoned various birth-control and contraceptive practices. In rejecting the teaching of the Manicheans, the Roman Church explicitly strengthened its rules discouraging sex without procreation, and further idealized virginity and self-restraint in marital relations. Further validation of these ideals occurred when a former follower of Mani converted to the Roman Church and, with the zeal characteristic of the religious convert, thoroughly repudiated his earlier-held Manichean beliefs. Augustine, subsequently canonized, condemned all forms of contraception including the rhythm method, a prohibition which remained in effect for sixteen centuries.

In the twelfth and thirteenth centuries rival ideologies again appeared to pose a threat to traditional Church teaching. The Cathars and the Troubadours, groups patronized by wealthy and important people of the times, were opposed to marriage and children as an outcome of sexual activity: pure love, they proclaimed, was an end in itself, a beautiful and meaningful human relationship. Reaction to these views by the Church resulted in the now familiar opposition to "artificial" contraception, an opposition finally weakened by the secular demands of responsible parenthood, leading to final removal of the opposition by most of the Protestant denominations in the 1930s, though officially remaining in effect today according to the Roman Catholic Church.

Despite official Catholic opposition to effective contraception, it is important to stress that Catholicism nevertheless in theory shares fully in the Judeo-Christian ethic which favours responsible parenthood. The Papal encyclical, *Humanae Vitae* (1968), although continuing to stress official opposition to artificial means of birth control, includes the principle that, with respect to procreation, "husband and wife recognize fully their own duties toward God, toward themselves, toward the family and toward society in a correct hierarchy of values."

In fact it is doubtful if statements from Rome on contraception are of direct importance today for, following the appearance of the reactionary and largely unexpected encyclical message, conferences of Catholic hierarchies in several countries, including Canada, went on record to soften its impact, for example: "In accord with the accepted principles of moral theology, if these persons have tried sincerely but without success to pursue a line of conduct in keeping with the [Papal] directive, they may be safely assured that whoever honestly chooses that course which seems right to him does so in good conscience" (from the *Statement of the Canadian Bishops on the Encyclical Humanae Vitae* (1968); for world-wide reaction to the encyclical, see Joannes 1970).

Apart from past (and for some, persistent) religious opposition to antinatalistic behaviour, there are important secular modes which work to perpetuate high levels of fertility in contemporary society. It is these social arrangements and secular beliefs which, if modified, promise a significant reduction in population growth.

Two social decisions that exert very great effects on population fertility are: to enter marriage, and to have a child. It is important to remember that individual freedom in respect to both these events is already institutionally controlled in our society as in all other human societies. The present legal age of marriage is already outmoded, reflecting an economic era long since past. Raising the legal age of marriage (to eighteen years for a female, in the judgement of the Royal Commission on the Status of Women) would likely lead to a greater reduction in fertility than the mere percentage of teenage marriage might suggest, for a disproportionately greater contribution to marital fertility is made by the younger age groups. To be socially (and hence politically) acceptable, especially among the youth of this country, the present-day unrealistic and unenlightened exclusion of unmarried clients from public birth-control programs needs revision. If the goal of population policies is truly to be social betterment, then any schemes purporting to serve that end must surely not discriminate harshly or unduly against any segment of the benefitting society. The facts of life, in respect to changed sexual behaviour and mores, stare us in the face; school, medical, social, and church authorities are only too aware of this reality, and theirs is perhaps the greater responsibility in bringing about social reformation to ensure that facilities provided under present-day legislation are truly available to all members of our society in known, or potential, need of preventive health care.

Social policies which encourage either late marriage or non-marriage will serve to reduce the incremental growth of population. The main negative effects of non-marriage must therefore be identified and counteracted. For example, social isolation and potential loss of social mobility, childlessness, and lack of economic support suffered by unmarried women are all powerful incentives to seek marriage. Provision of equally powerful rewards in the non-familial sphere could go some way toward reducing, or even obviating, the penalties incurred by non-marriage. Easier child adoption by qualified unmarried adults, special opportunities in high-status employment for single persons, prestigious communal housing for single persons (or one-parent families), and equitable insurance or taxation rates for unmarried persons are positive ways in which marital fertility may be reduced in a socially beneficial manner. Not only would population growth be reduced, but an otherwise potentially (or actually) socially disadvantaged segment of society would be afforded the opportunity to participate more fully in the mainstream of social and economic activity.

Insofar as population growth is in large part determined by the extent of the conscious desire of adults to produce children, it is important to understand fully (in a way we do not now) what needs a child fulfils in his parents, and to allow, wherever possible, institutional alternatives to satisfy or obviate those felt needs. This matter has been discussed at length (for example, Blake 1965), and herewith is a summary of my comments on the subject elsewhere (Freeman 1970).

Firstly, note again that social scientists have come to believe that what behaviour is repeated depends less on values and internal states (which tend to be conservative forces) and more on whether particular kinds of conduct are consistently and realistically rewarded. In such a view, then, the rewards (especially) and sanctions that a society offers can be important means of obtaining compliance with new societal goals.

Secondly, take the pressure off young people to enter into marriage early in their adult lives; certain counter-productive contributions of our present educational system have been referred to in Chapter 6.

Thirdly, remember that, given the choice, societies apparently reduce fertility by selecting means that involve the least institutional reform and the least human cost. It is unrealistic then to endeavour to promote such causes as celibacy, delayed marriage with chastity outside of marriage, or abstinence inside of marriage as means of reducing fertility.

Fourthly, recognize the continued need to expand the efficiency, provision, and awareness of the full range of birth-control measures available to all Canadians in need of such services; in that way they can responsibly conform to reproductive norms consonant with optimum individual health and national social and demographic goals.

Fifthly, initiate a variety of social changes which effectively decrease the dependence that adults place on child-producing as a means of self-validation or otherwise attaining or satisfying certain individual psychological or social ends.

Sixthly, and growing out of the fifth comment above (which seeks to establish children as ends in themselves rather than means of attaining adults' goals), increase national concern for the value of every child born, reflected in the best medical care, educational and occupational opportunities for each individual.

Lastly, and to a great extent involving a synthesis of the above reasons by way of emphasis, create by conscious design a Canadian society in which no unwanted child is born, and in which the decision to produce (as distinct from the decision to conceive) a child is made solely by the potential parents, and, furthermore, in which decisions about child-bearing are made in the social context that defines a three-child family as large.

EPILOGUE

Noted environmentalist David Brower has provided an apt analogy of mankind's present circumstances, where for some people of clear vision the end of the road is already in sight, even if the actual moment of ultimate tragedy remains obscure. The analogy does not stress the inevitability of the tragedy, but rather the uncertainty surrounding the situation. Consider, says Brower, that we are driving on a highway, and at every set interval of time we double our speed. At the outset, neither the acceleration nor the velocity are of concern: from one to two miles per hour, then to four, then eight, and so on—sixteen, thirty-two, and still we are comfortable and the situation is under control. The jump from thirty-two to sixty-four is a bit abrupt, but the vehicle can take it and the road is also designed for such a speed. Suddenly though, we begin to feel nervous—at 128 miles per hour events happen very quickly and we cannot take our eyes off the road nor our hands off the wheel. All our attention and energies must be given to the task of keeping on the road, and the trip is not so pleasurable now, even if rather exhilarating; at these speeds:

> We should feel nervous. We should be hearing sirens. We *are* nervous, and we are hearing sirens in the concern already voiced during . . . discussions, in the newspaper, and magazines, on television. All these are the sirens. But still many people think we can double again and speed up to 256 miles an hour. That is really happening. We have not gone off the road yet, but that does not mean we never will. (Brower 1970: 59.)

The fact is that we can go on doubling without any effort at all, by merely doing nothing, or we can slow down—not by running into some environmental obstruction (the ultimate and inevitable stopper) or by otherwise having a breakdown or accident of some type, but by exerting deliberate rational control over the powerful force that causes this runaway acceleration.

The analogy suggested by Brower can perhaps be usefully extended; who, we might ask, is to solve the particular problem he poses? We would be unwise to leave it to industry alone, for its solution would likely be to build more powerful cars so that the illusion of control and safety could be maintained at these breakneck speeds we are now travelling. Technologists also would likely find an unsatisfactory answer: they would seek to design highways which would allow us to travel with less probability of leaving the road despite the speed. What of government: would it merely advise that speed limits do exist, or post more signs to that effect and leave it to the individual to decide according to his or her conscience or commonsense whether to take heed?

It is possible that government would be really bold and exact stiff penalties from those who get caught, as a sort of deterrent (but as we all know, the probability of getting a speeding ticket is pretty low, especially if you are smart). It seems most unlikely that any of these groups would suggest anything that sounds like a control, a curb on the democratic right of all of us to enjoy the road as we see fit, even if that right is seriously threatening, not just ourselves, but all other road-users as well (even those who are on foot or on bicycles, for at these speeds an accident will surely have marked spill-overs, affecting all road-users).

It evidently does not require great vision or sagacity to advocate a slowing down of the machine; if, as seems to be the case, the machine goes that fast through ignorance of the causes and implications, then surely it is time for a massive dose of facts to dispel that unawareness. To formulate an adequate yet acceptable population policy for Canada will require exchange of a great deal of information, and, as that inevitably will take time, the less delay in starting the better. Undue speed, however, is not of the essence in regard to the formulation of a probable escape from the passive yet inexorable trend toward our ultimate collective undoing. We must deliberately and thoroughly formulate the propositions and gather the necessary facts and, then, in a systematic way consider and reflect upon and understand the *full* implication of acting, *or not acting,* against the trend.

A modest book such as this one need not aim to suggest in infinite and tedious detail what a population policy for Canada should or needs to be. Considerable dialogue and additional fact finding *must* necessarily precede any attempts at policy formulation, for otherwise it merely becomes an exercise in futility—yet another White Paper or Royal Commission tabled but never enacted, or perhaps enacted but never implemented. If recommendations of "experts" or legislative committees are not to become exercises in futility, they must be socially, politically, and administratively viable. If not, then members of society will ignore or subvert the intention of the reforms, or a ponderous bureaucracy will probably strangle the intent with red tape. As I believe we have far to travel yet before there is a sustained and critical public awareness of the issues and the range of possible solutions, this short book has attempted to place before the reader some of the many implications and determinants of our present population-related environmental predicament.

A recent book has warned us that in a culture such as ours, based on excess and overproduction, there results a steady and progressive loss of sharpness in our sensory awareness. Too many people and the commotion they create, together with the material plenitude they collectively manifest, conspire to dull our faculties (Sontag 1970:23). The inevitable result, unless we consciously seek to prevent it, is a partial awareness of what is happening around us to our world and to ourselves. In time we become overwhelmed by the sheer enormity and complexity of the task that, by default, has suddenly and belatedly come to our attention as requiring remedial action. Under such circumstances, confused reaction rather than constructive action is the more likely outcome. Poet Robert Graves contrasts the etiology and outcome of these two states:

He is quick, thinking in clear images;
I am slow, thinking in broken images.
He becomes dull, trusting to his clear images;
I become sharp, mistrusting my broken images.
Trusting his images, he assumes their relevance;

Mistrusting my images, I question their relevance.
Assuming their relevance, he assumes the fact;
Questioning their relevance, I question the fact.
When the fact fails him, he questions his senses;
When the fact fails me, I approve my senses.
He continues quick and dull in his clear images;
I continue slow and sharp in my broken images.
He in a confusion of his understanding;
I in a new understanding of my confusion.

What is presently of paramount importance to Canadian environment and society is a move toward ending the confusion that surrounds the role of population in the environmental crisis. The turmoil runs the gamut from all but ignoring population as a contributing factor to labelling it the primary cause of our environmental problems.

REFERENCES

ABRAMS, CHARLES
> 1968. Housing in the year 2000. In *Environment and policy: the next fifty years,* ed. W. R. Ewald, Jr., pp. 209–28. Bloomington: Indiana University Press.

ADAMSON, R.T.
> 1968. Housing policy and renewal. In *Urban studies: a Canadian perspective,* ed. N. H. Lithwick and Gilles Paquet, pp. 222–39. Toronto: Methuen.

ANON.
> 1971. Toward the year 2000: the ultimate goal of a population policy. *The Hastings Center Report* 3: 1–3.

ATLANTIC DEVELOPMENT BOARD
> 1969. *Urban centres in the Atlantic provinces.* A.D.B. Background Study No. 7. Ottawa: Queen's Printer.

AYRES, ROBERT U., and KNEESE, ALLEN V.
> 1971. Economic and ecological effects of a stationary population. *Annual Review of Ecology and Systematics* 2: 1–22.

BAILEY, ANTHONY
> 1969. Noise is a slow agent of death. *New York Times Magazine,* 23 November.

BARBOUR, IAN G.
> 1970a. *Science and secularity: the ethics of technology.* New York: Harper and Row Publishers.
> 1970b. An ecological ethic. In *Population crisis: an interdisciplinary perspective,* ed. Sue Titus Reid and David L. Lyon, pp. 72–78. Glenville, Illinois: Scott, Foresman and Company.

BARNETT, H. J.
>1971. Population problems: myths and realities. *Economic Development and Cultural Change* 19(4): 545–59.

BARNETT, LARRY D.
>1971. Zero Population Growth, Inc. *Bioscience* 21(14): 759–65.

BATES, DAVID V.
>1972. *A citizen's guide to air pollution.* Montreal: McGill–Queen's University Press.

BECK, M. B.
>1970. Abortion: the mental consequences of unwantedness. *Seminars in Psychiatry* 2: 263–74.

BERELSON, BERNARD
>1969. Beyond family planning. *Studies in Family Planning* 38: 1–16.

BERLE, A. A., JR.
>1968. What GNP doesn't tell us. *Saturday Review,* 31 August.

BERMAN, EDGAR
>1970. Human non-proliferation: a political responsibility. In *Agenda for survival: the environmental crisis–2,* ed. Harold W. Helfrich, Jr., pp. 15–36. New Haven: Yale University Press.

BLACKMAN, F. F.
>1905. Optima and limiting factors. *Annals of Botany* 19: 281–95.

BLAKE, JUDITH
>1965. Demographic science and the redirection of population policy. *Journal of Chronic Diseases* 18: 1181–1200.
>1969. Population policy for Americans: is the government being misled? *Science* 164: 522–29.
>1971. Reproductive motivation and population policy. *Bioscience* 21: 215–20.

BORGSTROM, GEORG
>1967. *Hungry Planet.* Toronto: Collier–Macmillan.
>1969. *Too Many.* Toronto: Collier–Macmillan.
>1970. The harvest of the seas: how fruitful and for whom? In *The environmental crisis: man's struggle to live with himself,* ed. Harold W. Helfrich, Jr., pp. 65–84. New Haven: Yale University Press.

BOULDING, KENNETH E.

- 1966. The economics of coming spaceship Earth. In *Environmental quality in a growing economy,* ed. H. Jarrett, pp. 3–14. Baltimore: Johns Hopkins University Press.
- 1970. Fun and games with the Gross National Product — the role of misleading indicators of social policy. In *The environmental crisis: man's struggle to live with himself,* ed. Harold W. Helfrich, Jr., pp. 157–70. New Haven: Yale University Press.

BROWER, DAVID

- 1970. The search for an environmental perspective. In *Agenda for survival: the environmental crisis — 2,* ed. Harold W. Helfrich, Jr., pp. 55–70. New Haven: Yale University Press.

BROWN, LESTER R.

- 1967. The world outlook for conventional agriculture. *Science* 158: 604–11.
- 1970. Human food production as a process in the biosphere. *Scientific American* 223(3): 160–70.
- 1971. The social impact of the Green Revolution. *International Conciliation,* No. 581.

BUMPASS, LARRY, and WESTOFF, CHARLES F.

- 1970. The "perfect contraceptive" population. *Science* 169: 1177–82.

CAIN, STANLEY A.

- 1967. Population ecology. *Alma College Perspective* 3(2): 27–31.

CALLAHAN, DANIEL

- 1972. Ethics and population limitation. *Science* 175: 477–86.

CALLWOOD, JUNE

- 1969. Impact of family planning in Canada. In *Exploding humanity: the crisis of numbers,* ed. Henry Regier and J. Bruce Falls, pp. 65–70. Toronto: Anansi.

CANADA

- 1971. *Current status of family planning in Canada.* Ottawa: Department of National Health and Welfare.

CANADA
: 1971. *Canada yearbook: 1970–71.* Ottawa: Dominion Bureau of Statistics.

CANADIAN BROADCASTING CORPORATION
: 1971. Public opinion in Canada on certain aspects of the law relating to abortion. Toronto: C.B.C. Research Department. mimeo.

CAPPON, DANIEL
: 1971. Mental health in the high-rise. *Canadian Journal of Public Health* 62(5): 426–31.

CHANT, DONALD A. (editor)
: 1970. *Pollution Probe.* Toronto: New Press.

CHASTEEN, EDGAR R.
: 1971. *The case for compulsory birth control.* Englewood Cliffs, N. J.: Prentice-Hall.

CLAMAN, A. DAVID; WAKEFORD, JOHN R.; TURNER, JOHN M. M.; and HAYDEN, BRIAN
: 1971. Impact on hospital practice of liberalizing abortions and female sterilizations. *Canadian Medical Association Journal* 105: 35–41.

CLARK, COLIN
: 1967. *Population growth and land use.* London: Macmillan.

CLOUD, PRESTON E., JR.
: 1968. Realities of mineral distribution. *Texas Quarterly* 11: 103–26.

COALE, ANSLEY, JR.
: 1968. Should the United States start a campaign for fewer births? *Population Index* 34(4): 467–74.
: 1970. Man and his environment. *Science* 170: 132–36.

COMMONER, BARRY
: 1967. *Science and survival.* New York: Viking.

COOKE, G. W.
: 1970. The carrying capacity of the land in the year 2000. In *The optimum population for Britain,* ed. L. R. Taylor, pp. 15–42. London: Academic Press.

CORBET, PHILIP S., and LEROUX, E. J.
: 1972. The population problem: a vital Canadian policy issue. *Science Forum* 5(1): 1,32.

DAVIS, KINGSLEY, and BLAKE, JUDITH
    1956. Social structure and fertility: an analytic framework. *Economic Development and Cultural Change* 4(3): 211–35.

DAY, LINCOLN H.
    1967. The population problem in the United States. In *The 99th hour: the population crisis in the United States,* ed. Daniel O. Price, pp. 53–70. Chapel Hill, N. C.: University of North Carolina Press.

DUNBAR, M. J.
    1971. *Environment and good sense.* Montreal: McGill–Queen's University Press.

EASTERLIN, R. A.
    1966. On the relation of economic factor to recent and projected fertility changes. *Demography* 3: 131–53.
    1969. Toward a socio-economic theory of fertility: a survey of recent research on economic factors in American fertility. In *Fertility and family planning: a world view,* ed. S. J. Behrman, L. Corsa, Jr., and R. Freedman, pp. 127–56. Ann Arbor: University of Michigan Press.

EHRENFELD, DAVID W.
    1970. *Biological conservation.* New York: Holt, Rinehart and Winston.

EHRLICH, PAUL R.
    1968. *The population bomb.* New York: Ballantyne.
    1970. Famine 1975: fact or fallacy? In *The environmental crisis: man's struggle to live with himself,* ed. Harold W. Helfrich, Jr., pp. 47–64. New Haven: Yale University Press.

EHRLICH, PAUL R., and EHRLICH, ANNE H.
    1970. *Population, resources, environment: issues in human ecology.* San Francisco: W. H. Freeman.

ELIOT, JOHAN W.
    1967. On the outer edge of family planning. *Alma College Perspective* 3(2): 46–62.

FREEDMAN, R., and COOMBS, L.
    1966. Economic considerations in family growth decisions. *Population Studies* 20: 197–222.

FREEMAN, MILTON M. R.

    1970. Not by bread alone: anthropological perspectives on optimum population. In *The optimum population for Britain,* ed. L. R. Taylor, pp. 139–49, 170–73. London: Academic Press.

    1971a. The significance of demographic changes occurring in the Canadian East Arctic. *Anthropologica,* N. S. 13: 215–36.

    1971b. The Utterly Dismal Theorem: a contemporary example from the Canadian East Arctic. Paper read at Annual Meeting, Canadian Sociology and Anthropology Association.

FREJKA, TOMAS

    1968. Reflections on the demographic conditions needed to establish a United States stationary population growth. *Population Studies* 22(3): 379–97.

FYE, P. M.; MAXWELL, A. E.; EMERY, K. O.; and KETCHUM, B. H.

    1968. Ocean science and marine resources. In *Uses of the seas,* ed. Edmund A. Gullion, pp. 17–68. Englewood Cliffs, N. J.: Prentice-Hall.

GALBRAITH, J. K.

    1964. Economics and the quality of life. *Science* 145: 117–23.

GERSHINOWITZ, HAROLD

    1972. Applied research for the public good — a suggestion. *Science* 176: 380–86.

GILLEN, MOLLIE

    1970. Why women are still angry over abortion. *Chatelaine,* October 1970.

GLACKEN, CLARENCE J.

    1970. Man against nature: an outmoded concept. In *The environmental crisis: man's struggle to live with himself,* ed. Harold W. Helfrich, Jr., pp. 127–42. New Haven: Yale University Press.

GRIFFIN, K. B.

    1969. Choice, institutions and technology: an economist's impressions. In *Intermediate adaptation in Newfoundland and the Arctic: a strategy of social and economic development,* ed. Milton M. R. Freeman, pp. 89–96. St. John's, Newfoundland: Institute of Social and Economic Research.

HAMMOND, R. PHILIP
> 1970. Energy: the ultimate raw material. *Science* 167: 1439.

HARDIN, GARRETT
> 1968a. Abortion—or compulsory pregnancy. *Journal of Marriage and the Family* 30: 246–51.
> 1968b. The tragedy of the commons. *Science* 162: 1243–48.
> 1969a. *Population, evolution and birth control: a collage of controversial ideas.* 2nd edition. San Francisco: W. H. Freeman.
> 1969b. Dick and Jane: what is pornography? In *Population, evolution and birth control: a collage of controversial ideas,* ed. Garrett Hardin, pp. 312–14. San Francisco: W. H. Freeman.

HARRIS, MARVIN
> 1966. The cultural ecology of India's sacred cattle. *Current Anthropology* 7: 51–66.

HAWTHORN, GEOFFREY P.
> 1970a. *The sociology of fertility.* London: Collier–Macmillan.
> 1970b. Some social consequences of growing numbers. In *The optimum population for Britain,* ed. L. R. Taylor, pp. 59–69. London: Academic Press.

HENRIPIN, JACQUES
> 1968. *Tendances et facteurs de la fécondité au Canada.* Ottawa: Dominion Bureau of Statistics.

HOLDREN, JOHN P., and EHRLICH, PAUL R. (editors)
> 1971. *Global ecology: readings toward a rational strategy for man.* New York: Harcourt Brace Jovanovich, Inc.

HOLT, S. J.
> 1969. The food resources of the ocean. *Scientific American* 221(3): 178–94.

HUXLEY, JULIAN S.
> 1963. *The human crisis.* Seattle: University of Washington Press.

JOANNES, VITTORINO (editor)
> 1970. *The bitter pill.* Philadelphia: Pilgrim Press.

KAHN, HERMAN, and WEINER, ANTHONY
> 1969. *The year 2000.* New York: Macmillan.

KALBACH, WARREN E., and MCVEY, WAYNE W.
>1971. *The demographic bases of Canadian society.* Toronto: McGraw-Hill.

KANGAS, LENNI W.
>1970. Integrated incentives for fertility control. *Science* 169: 1278–83.

KEENLEYSIDE, HUGH
>1969. Canada's role in the world population crisis. In *Exploding humanity: the crisis of numbers,* ed. Henry Regier and J. Bruce Falls, pp. 155–62. Toronto: Anansi.

KETCHEL, MELVIN M.
>1968. Fertility control agents as a possible solution to the world population problem. *Perspectives in Biology and Medicine* 11(4): 687–703.

LADEJINSKY, WOLF
>1970. Ironies of India's Green Revolution. *Foreign Affairs* 48(4): 758–68.

LADER, LAWRENCE
>1966. *Abortion.* Boston: Beacon Press.

LEDERER, WILLIAM J., and BURDICK, EUGENE
>1958. *The Ugly American.* New York: Norton.

LÉGARÉ, JACQUES, and HENRIPIN, JACQUES
>1971. Recent trends in Canadian fertility. *Canadian Review of Sociology and Anthropology* 8(2): 106–18.

LEIBENSTEIN, H.
>1957. *Economic backwardness and economic growth.* New York: Wiley.

LEKACHMAN, ROBERT
>1971. Humanizing G.N.P. *Social Policy* 2(3): 34–39.

MACARTHUR, ROBERT, and CONNELL, JOSEPH
>1966. *The biology of populations.* New York: John Wiley.

MACNEILL, J. W.
>1971. *Environmental management.* Constitutional study prepared for the Government of Canada. Ottawa: Information Canada.

MAEOTS, KRISTA
>1970. Abortion caravan. *Canadian Forum,* August, 1970.

MARINE, GENE
    1970. The California water plan: the most expensive faucet in the world. *Ramparts,* May, pp. 36–41.

MARTIN, A. R.
    1964. Man's leisure and his health. *Bulletin of the New York Academy of Medicine* 40(1): 21–42.

MAYER, JEAN
    1964. Food and population: the wrong problem? *Daedalus* 93(3): 830–44.

MCLACHLAN, GORDON (editor)
    1971. *Patient, doctor, society.* Oxford: Oxford University Press.

MCLENNAN, R. E.
    1972. Is abortion immoral? *Ferment '68* 1(4): 4–7; 15.

MCROBIE, G.
    1969. Intermediate technology and development. In *Intermediate adaptation in Newfoundland and the Arctic: a strategy of social and economic development,* ed. Milton M. R. Freeman, pp. 8–20. St. John's, Newfoundland: Institute of Social and Economic Research.

MCTAGGART COWAN, IAN
    1969. Ecology and discretion. In *Exploding humanity: the crisis of numbers,* ed. Henry Regier and J. Bruce Falls, pp. 141–53. Toronto: Anansi.

MILES, RUFUS E., JR.
    1970. Whose baby is the population problem? *Population Bulletin* 26(1): 3–36.

MISHAN, E. J.
    1969. The spillover enemy: the coming struggle for amenity rights. *Encounter* 33(6): 3–13.

MITCHELL, E. R.
    1971. *Only people pollute.* Canada, Department of Energy, Mines and Resources, Mines Branch, Information Circular LC 268. Ottawa: Information Canada.

MONCRIEF, LEWIS W.
    1970. The cultural basis for our environmental crisis. *Science* 170: 508–12.

MORGAN, FRANK
- 1970. *Pollution: Canada's critical challenge.* Toronto: Ryerson/Maclean–Hunter.

MURPHEY, RHOADS
- 1967. Man and nature in China. *Modern Asian Studies* 1(4): 313–33.

MUSSON, PATRICIA
- 1971. Infant mortality in Canada. In *Population issues in Canada,* ed. Carl F. Grindstaff, Craig L. Boydell, and Paul C. Whitehead, pp. 60–67. Toronto: Holt, Rinehart and Winston.

NOONAN, JOHN T.
- 1965. *Contraception.* Cambridge, Mass.: Harvard University Press.

NORTMAN, D.
- 1971. Population and family planning programs: a factbook. *Reports on Population/Family Planning,* 2.

NORTON–TAYLOR, D.
- 1966. What the United States can do about world hunger. *Fortune,* June.

NOTESTEIN, FRANK W.
- 1970. Zero population growth. *Population Index* 36(4): 444–52.

O'DONNELL, MICHAEL
- 1970. Dublin's lonely outpost. *World Medicine* 5(10): 17–23.

ODUM, EUGENE P.
- 1969. The strategy of ecosystem development. *Science* 164: 262–70.

OTTOSSON, JAN–OTTO
- 1971. Legal abortion in Sweden: thirty years' experience. *Journal of Biosocial Science* 3: 173–92.

PADDOCK, W. C.
- 1970. How green is the Green Revolution? *Bioscience* 20(16): 897–902.

PADDOCK, WILLIAM, and PADDOCK, PAUL
- 1964. *Hungry nations.* Boston: Little, Brown and Company.
- 1967. *Famine—1975!* Boston: Little, Brown and Company.

PARKES, A. S.

   1970. The doctor's dilemma, 1970. In *The optimum population for Britain,* ed. L. R. Taylor, pp. 49–58. London: Academic Press.

PEARL, ARTHUR, and PEARL, STEPHANIE

   1971. Toward an ecological theory of value. *Social Policy* 2(1): 30–33, 37–38.

PELRINE, ELEANOR WRIGHT

   1971. *Abortion in Canada.* Toronto: New Press.

POTTER, RALPH B., JR.

   1967. Protestant parochialism and the population problem. *Alma College Perspective* 3(2): 6–14.

   1969. *Updating life and death.* Boston: Beacon Press.

   1971. The abortion debate. In *The survival equation: man, resources and his environment,* ed. Roger Revelle, Ashok Khosla, and Maris Vinorskis, pp. 91–107. Boston: Houghton, Mifflin.

POTTER, ROBERT G.

   1971. Inadequacy of a one-method family planning program. *Studies in Family Planning* 2(1): 1–5.

   1972. Additional births averted when abortion is added to contraception. *Studies in Family Planning* 3(4): 53–59.

PRICE, DANIEL O. (editor)

   1967. *The 99th hour: the population crisis in the United States.* Chapel Hill, N. C.: University of North Carolina Press.

QUERIDO, A.

   1964. Population problems and mental health. In *Population and mental health,* ed. H. P. David, pp. 29–39. New York: Springer.

RAMSEY, JAMES

   1969. Wonderland revisited. *Sierra Club Bulletin* 54(10): 10–13.

RAO, KAMARAZU NARASIMHA

   1969. Population and public health. In *Exploding humanity: the crisis of numbers,* ed. Henry Regier and J. Bruce Falls, pp. 105–13, 134. Toronto: Anansi.

REGIER, HENRY, and FALLS, J. BRUCE (editors)

   1969. *Exploding humanity: the crisis of numbers.* Toronto: Anansi.

REID, ROBERT
    1972. Hypocrisy and Hippocrates. *The Listener,* 30 March.

RUDD, ROBERT
    1964. *Pesticides and the living landscape.* Madison: University of Wisconsin Press.

RYTHER, JOHN H.
    1969. Photosynthesis and fish production in the sea. *Science* 166: 72–76.

SCIENCE COUNCIL OF CANADA
    1970. *Annual report 1969–70.* Ottawa: Information Canada.
    1971. *Annual report 1970–71.* Ottawa: Information Canada.

SEARS, PAUL B.
    1935. *Deserts on the march.* Norman: University of Oklahoma Press.

SEGAL, SHELDON J., and TIETZE, CHRISTOPHER
    1971. Contraceptive technology: current and prospective methods. *Reports on Population/Family Planning,* July.

SIMMS, M., and MEDEWAR, J.
    1970. How much pressure on the individual? In *The optimum population for Britain,* ed. L. R. Taylor, pp. 131–38. London: Academic Press.

SIMMONS, A.
    1971. York family study. Department of Sociology and Anthropology, York University. Toronto, mimeo.

SMITH, HARMON L.
    1971. Abortion, death and the sanctity of life. *Social Science and Medicine* 5(3): 211–18.

SMITH, L. K.
    1970. Noise as a pollutant. *Canadian Journal of Public Health* 61(6): 475–80.

SNOW, C. P.
    1961. What is the world's greatest need? *New York Times Magazine,* 2 April.

SONTAG, SUSAN
    1970. *Against interpretation.* New York: Dell Publishing Co.

SORVALL, VIVIAN
- 1971. *Overpopulation: how many are too many?* West Haven, Conn.: Pendulum Press.

SPENGLER, JOSEPH J.
- 1966. Values and fertility analysis. *Demography* 3(1): 109–30.
- 1967. The costs of population growth. *Alma College Perspective* 3(2): 32–38.
- 1969. Population problems: in search of a solution. *Science* 166: 1234–38.

STANFORD, QUENTIN H. (editor)
- 1972. *The world's population: problems of growth.* Toronto: Oxford University Press.

STYCOS, J. M.
- 1963. Obstacles to programs of population control—facts and fancies. *Marriage and Family Living* 25: 5–13.

SUZUKI, DAVID T.
- 1970. Is a technological society really compatible with human dignity? *Science Forum* 3(5): 3–6.

THOMAS, W. D. S.
- 1968. Maternal mortality in native British Columbian Indians, a high-risk group. *Canadian Medical Association Journal* 99: 64–67.

TIETZE, CHRISTOPHER, and LEWIT, SARAH
- 1972. Joint program for the study of abortion (JPSA): early medical complications of legal abortion. *Studies in Family Planning* 3(6): 97–122.

UNITED NATIONS
- 1969. Problems of the human environment: report of the Secretary-General. United Nations Economic and Social Council, Document E/4667, 47th Session.

UDALL, STEWART L.
- 1970. Total environment: a new political reality. In *Agenda for survival: the environmental crisis—2,* ed. Harold W. Helfrich, Jr., pp. 1–13. New Haven: Yale University Press.

VEATCH, ROBERT M.
- 1972. Updating the Hippocratic oath. *Medical Opinion* 8(2): 56–61.

VEEVERS, J. E.
  1971. The liberalization of Canadian abortion laws. In *Population issues in Canada,* ed. Carl F. Grindstaff, Craig L. Boydell, and Paul C. Whitehead, pp. 33–39. Toronto: Holt, Rinehart and Winston.

WALLACE, BRUCE
  1972. *People, their needs, environment ecology. Essays on social biology.* Volume 1. Englewood Cliffs, N. J.: Prentice-Hall.

WEEDON, R. B., and KLEIN, D. R.
  1971. Wildlife and oil: a survey of critical issues in Alaska. *Polar Record* 15(97):479–94.

WESTELL, ANTHONY
  1971. Why we can't wait for evolution. *Vancouver Sun,* 10 July.

WESTOFF, LESLIE ALDRIDGE, and WESTOFF, CHARLES F.
  1968. *From now to zero: fertility, contraception and abortion in America.* Boston: Little, Brown.

WILLIAMSON, F. S. L.
  1969. Population pollution. *Bioscience* 19(11): 979–83.

WOODWELL, G. M.
  1967. Toxic substances and ecologic cycles. *Scientific American* 216(3): 24–31.

YATES, WILSON
  1971. *Family planning on a crowded planet.* Minneapolis: Ausburg Publishing House.

ADDENDUM

In the field of national and international development, several essays have recently appeared which attempt to promote the idea of development based on a "no-growth" model, rather than a continuation of present growth-oriented schemes based on the current western industrial model. The classic essay exploring the various implications of our current practices is:

MEADOWS, DONNELLA H.; MEADOWS, DENNIS L.;
RANDERS, JØRGEN; AND BEHRENS, WILLIAM W., III
1972. *The limits to growth.* New York: New American Library.

> Using a simulation modelling approach, the authors conclude that the limits to growth (of population, resource consumption, food production, and pollution) will be reached within a century, and that the most probable outcome will be a rather sudden and uncontrollable decline in both population and industrial capacity. (For a critical review of some inadequacies in the methodology however, see Schwartz, S. I., and Foin, T. C. 1972, in *Human Ecology* 1 (2): 161–73.)

Other recent writings pertinent to the concerns of this volume include the following:

CANADIAN COMMISSION FOR U.N.E.S.C.O.
1972. *Economic development and human survival.*
Occasional Paper No. 3.

> Starting with the premise that environmental stress is the product of three main factors, namely, population, social organization (lifestyle), and technology, the authors of

the paper urge a search for, and acceptance of, no-growth models of development.

CHANT, D. A. and REGIER, H. A.
1972. A challenge to the traditional western view of development. *Science Forum* 5 (5): 3–6.

A strong plea for reform among the developed nations in regard to environment-threatening development activities, so as to provide models for the less-developed nations to adopt.

HENDERSON, HAZEL
1973. Ecologists versus economists. *Harvard Business Review* 51 (4): 28–30, 152–57.

A very useful review of recent seminal and innovative ideas concerned with rationalizing environmentally inappropriate decision-making in business and government. Includes reference to recent writings of Boulding, Commoner, Forrester, Kapp, and H. T. Odum (see Kierans in *Canadian Forum,* June–July 1973, and Franson 1973 for some Canadian perspectives on this topic).

Ontario Naturalist, 13 (1), 1973 includes three papers pertinent to, and extolling, the no-growth ethic: renowned Canadian architect Raymond Moriyama writes on growth, temporal and spiritual; Garrett Hardin on population limitation, and Ian McHarg on design with nature.

SCIENCE COUNCIL OF CANADA
1973a. *Annual report 1972–73.* Ottawa: Information Canada.

The first report of the Council since the new chairman took office. It is significant that the concerns of the previous chairman in regard to population matters are not reflected in the statements of his successor, and that the population research project now contemplated by the council will be of very limited scope, namely to look at the effects present and future technology may have on population and demographic trends in Canada.

1973b. *Natural resources policy in Canada.* Report Number 19, Science Council of Canada. Ottawa: Information Canada.

Views Canada in a global as well as national context, and recommends a transition from a consumer society to a conserver society, which though not contributing to a net decrease in annual consumption of resources would result in a net decrease in the rate of growth of resource consumption.

REGIER, HENRY A.; FALLS, J. BRUCE; and TAYLOR, CHRIS E.
1973. The population factor in the environmental equation. In *A population policy for Canada?* Toronto: Conservation Council of Ontario and the Family Planning Federation of Canada.

An ecologic analysis, by a team of University of Toronto scientists, of the development–population–environment equation, which concludes that due to the multiplier effect of population and the inefficiencies of the industrial process, population growth is a luxury the global ecosystem can no longer afford.

WILSON, J. T.
1973. International research. In *Science and the North.* Ottawa: Information Canada.

(See Wilson's articles in *Maclean's,* March 1973, and Toronto *Globe and Mail,* 14 August 1973.) Geophysicist and president of the Royal Society of Canada, the author argues for husbanding of Canada's non-renewable resources by adoption of policies which will look to and effectively safeguard energy requirements for future generations. For a fuller exploration of Canada's resource policy deficiencies the reader is referred to articles in the June–July 1973 issue of *Canadian Forum* and three recent books in particular:

RICHARDSON, BOYCE
1972. *James Bay: the plot to drown the northwoods.* Toronto: Clark, Irwin.

ROHMER, RICHARD
1973. *The arctic imperative: an overview of the energy crisis.* Toronto: McClelland and Stewart.

WOODFORD, JAMES
1974. *The Inuvik conspiracy.* Toronto: McClelland and Stewart.

Issues related to population policy in Canada and in other similarly developed nations have been explored in several recent works, the most comprehensive of which, relating to Canada is:

MARSDEN, LORNA
1973. *Population probe: Canada.* Toronto: Copp Clark.

The following are also pertinent:

BARRETT, F. MICHAEL, and FITZ-EARLE, MALCOLM
1973a. Should Canada withhold aid from developing countries lacking population control? *Science Forum* 6(2): 3–6.

> Using the text of a brief delivered to a Parliamentary Standing Committee in 1971, and excerpts from replies to certain of their statements, the authors stress the urgency of developing a national policy.

BERELSON, BERNARD
1973. Formulation of a population policy. *Perspectives in Biology and Medicine* 16 (3): 446–56.

> The president of the Population Council, New York, writes of the increased awareness and need for population policies among the highly developed nations of the western world, and authoritatively emphasizes the holistic and pervasive nature of the task of formulating and implementing such proposals.

BROWN, GEORGE F.
1972. *Population policy and national development.* IDRC Report 007e. Ottawa: International Development Research Centre.

> An address by the director, Population and Health Sciences Division of IDRC, to a council meeting of the International Planned Parenthood Federation held in Ottawa, May 1972. The Canadian government approach is viewed as low-key.

BROWN, G., and MARSON, WENDY K.
1973. Consideration of a population policy for Canada. In *A population policy for Canada?* Toronto: Ontario Conservation Council and the Family Planning Federation of Canada.

A discussion of the implications of certain demographic trends in Canada, illustrating the degree to which population issues affect many aspects of national life.

COMMISSION ON POPULATION GROWTH AND THE AMERICAN FUTURE
1972. *Population growth and the American future.* Washington, D.C.: Government Printing Office (also published in New York: New American Library).

A comprehensive look at the pattern and implications of population behaviour in the United States which serves as model for a national population enquiry. However, despite being soundly researched and written by concerned commissioners, it seems probable that many of the more important recommendations will be ignored by government (see Piotrow 1973).

Family Planning and Population. Quarterly Newsletter. Toronto: Family Planning Federation of Canada.

A new newsletter, first published in Spring 1973, reporting on recent developments in the population field in Canada. The first issue included a report that at the Annual Meeting of the Federation in December 1972 a resolution was passed urging the federal government to develop a national population policy. As part of that resolve, the federation is to establish a population division with emphasis on research and information in the demography and population fields.

FRANSON, ROBERT T.
1973. Governmental secrecy in Canada. *Nature Canada* 2 (2): 31–34.

This analysis, by a University of British Columbia law professor, indicates the degree to which the Canadian government excludes public involvement in influencing the decision-making process. (See articles by Page,

Thompson and Crommelin, McDougall, and Pimlott in *Canadian Forum,* June–July 1973.)

PIOTROW, PHYLLIS T.
1973. *World population crisis: the United States response.* New York: Praeger.

Although presenting an analysis of United States governmental policy toward birth control, both in national and international programs, this book has discussion of relevance to Canada too, on the role of public opinion and debate, private organizations, and the legal and legislative systems in effecting change in official policy. (However, see Franson 1973 and Hellman 1973.)

In the sections of this volume relating to Canadian attitudes and practice in regard to birth control there remains a regrettable absence of good data, and a consequent need therefore to present material relating more directly to non-Canadian societies. Recently published material on Canada, other than that referred to in *Population Probe: Canada* by Dr. Lorna Marsden, includes the following:

BALAKRISHNAN, T. R.; ROSS, SHAN; ALLINGHAM, JOHN D.; and KANTNER, JOHN F.
1972. Attitudes toward abortion of married women in metropolitan Toronto. *Social Biology* 19 (1): 35–42.

The results of a survey among 1632 Toronto women prior to changes in the abortion laws. Religious affiliation was found to be the strongest indicator of attitude toward abortion, with religiosity also an important variable. Authors concluded that a decline in religious values would contribute to a more liberal attitude toward abortion. The survey also found a discrepancy between the stated attitude and the probable action in respect to abortion in the women interviewed. (See also Barrett and Fitz-Earle 1973 and Schwenger 1973 for more recent surveys in Canada.)

BARRETT, F. MICHAEL, and FITZ-EARLE, MALCOLM
1973b. Student opinion on legalized abortion at the University of Toronto. *Canadian Journal of Public Health* 64 (3): 294–99.

Comparison of the results of surveys conducted in 1969 and 1971 indicate an increasing proportion of students favour abortion when pregnancy has resulted from each of six different circumstances. The responses are broken down according to sex and religion of respondent. (For an assessment of the degree to which religiosity (devoutness) affects Canadian responses, see Greenglass, in Schlesinger 1973; see also material in Orton 1973 and in Westoff and Bumpass 1973 and Balakrishnan *et al.* 1972).

HELLMAN, LOUIS M.

1973. Conception control as a health practice: an emerging concept in government and medicine. *Perspectives in Biology and Medicine* 16 (3): 357–68.

The author, a high-ranking official in the United States government responsible for population affairs, provides an excellent discussion of the medical and social benefits resulting from an effective public health program of birth control. Though using United States material, this paper has material pertinent to any consideration of health problems in the remoter regions of Canada.

ORTON, MAUREEN (editor)

1973. *Human sexuality and fertility services — social policy and social work education.* Ottawa: Canadian Association of Schools of Social Work.

The papers and reports of workshops at a symposium held in November 1972. Some papers provide new empirical data in respect to birth control behaviour of Canadians.

SCHWENGER, COPE W.

1973. Abortion in Canada as a public health problem and a community health measure. *Canadian Journal of Public Health* 64 (3): 223–30

A thorough analysis of changing abortion practices in Canada since amendment of the Criminal Code in August 1969. Decrease in illegal abortion, reduced maternal mortality and morbidity rates, decrease in incidence of high-risk pregnancy resulting in lowered neonatal and perinatal mortality rates are all apparent in statistical tables. The article also illustrates the inequities of the present arrangements however, with it appearing to be 30 times as difficult to obtain an abortion in Newfoundland as in British Columbia.

SCHLESINGER, B. (editor)
1974. *Family planning in Canada.* Toronto: University of Toronto Press.
A collection of papers bringing together results of studies on the subject. The editor teaches an innovative course on family planning and social work at the University of Toronto.

WESTOFF, CHARLES F., and BUMPASS, LARRY
1973. The revolution in birth control practices of United States Roman Catholics. *Science* 179: 41–49.

Given the political activity of the Catholic population in Canada, this paper is germane, notwithstanding its attention to the American social scene. Surveys indicate that the more educated Catholics are becoming more like non-Catholics in their attitudes toward birth control. Increased rejection of Church proscriptions in regard to contraception is quite prevalent among those still "active" in their religion; the authors suggest this is indicative of a profound sociological change which has generated tensions within Catholicism that can only result in a change in Church doctrine. (See also Barrett and Fitz–Earle 1973b, and Guyatt in Orton 1973.)

INDEX

Abortion, 102–9, 141–43; in Nova Scotia, 80; and sex education, 102; and the Canadian criminal code, 103; Vancouver Women's Caucus on, 104; justifiable, 106; Protestant view on, 105, 106, 109; and contraception, 106; conflicting views on, 107, 142; frequency of, 108; and the needs of the state, 109; historical determinants of, 141; dangers of, 142; role of, in population control, 143
Age distribution in Canada, 74–77
Agriculture: in India, 34–36; modernization in, 38, 42, 44; and biogeochemical cycles, 43; and total land surface, 43; and introduction of foreign crops, 44; and selective breeding, 44; and use of DDT, 47; organization and food supply, 50
Amino acids, 40
Automobiles, 22, 25

Bacon, Francis, 93
Baird, Sir Dugal, 129
Baldwin, James, 57
Beans, 41
Bernard, G., 90
Biocides, 47, 48
Biogeochemical cycles, 43
Biosphere, 58
Biotic diversity, 48
Birds, extermination of, 47
Birth control: and abortion, 108; credibility of programs of, 108; and Criminal Code of Canada, 131; and Biblical sanctions, 145; Catholic Church on, 131, 145–47; and Judeo–Christian ethics, 146
Blackman, F. E., 33
Boulding, Kenneth, 2, 90, 96
Bridges, Robert, 1

Calgary, Alberta, 17
Calorie yields, 42
Canadian Society of Wildlife and Fishery Biologists: on population policy, 84–85
Carbon monoxide concentrations, 24
Catholic views: on abortion, 105; on birth control, 145
Catholic bishops of Canada: brief to Commons Committee on Health and

Welfare, 131
Cereal, yields in Britain, 46
Chant, Donald A., 78
Child, cost to the State, in Canada, 129–30
Cobourg, Ontario, 18
Contraception, 119; methods of, 108, 109, 144, 145. *See also* Birth control
Cooke, G. W., 46
Crop rotation, 46
Cows: value of, in India, 38, 39; and milk production, 44
Crude birth rate: and population fertility, 63–64; in Canada, 117
Cultural norms: and pollution, 4; and destruction of endangered species, 56; and family size, 124–25
Cycles: biogeochemical, 43; hydrological, 54, 55

Density, population, 5, 79. *See also* Urbanization
Dover, Thomas, 90
Durkheim, Emil, 3
Demographic considerations: and family size, 116–18; and reproductive control, 102

Ecologic: definition of, 7
Economic: growth, 26–27; model, 123; status and fertility, 126–27
Edmonton, Alberta, 17
Education and normative behaviour, 127–28
Egg production, 44
Ehrenfeld, David, 56, 57
Ehrlich, Paul, 3, 47
Eisenhower, Dwight D., 131
Energy transfer, 40–41, 42
Entomological Society of Canada, 83–84
Environmental crisis: global nature of, 97; and the abortion conflict, 107

Erie, Lake, 10, 47
Estrus, 100
Ethics and personal choice, 96

Family planning, 80–81; Government report on current status of, in Canada, 110–11, 112
Family size: and urbanization, 64; and population increase, 64; trends in, 75, 116, 119; ideals held re, 117; and zero population growth, 118; demographic considerations of, 116–18; sociological considerations of, 118–22; economic considerations of, 122–24; and cultural norms, 124–25; motivational aspects of, 124–26
Fertility: and economic activity, 63; factors in decline of, 65; control and Canadian law, 80; social determinants of, 119; rates and national policy, 120; trends, predictions in, 127; means of reducing, 148, 149. *See also* Government intercession
Fertilizers, 34, 39, 46, 47
Fishing, 49–50, 52, 53
Freedom, personal, 96, 98, 99, 100, 132
Food: consumption and production, 32, 36, 37; supply, global nature of, 38

Gandhi, Mahatma, 39
Government: report on Current Status of Family Planning in Canada, 110–11, 112; intercession and fertility control, 128–35, 137
Grain: production, 36; consumption, comparative data on, 37

INDEX 179

Graves, Robert, 152
Green Revolution, The, 32, 35, 38, *passim*
Gross National Product, 25, 61; world figures, 25; and gross national cost, 26; limitations of, 28–30
Growth efficiency, 40, 41
Gut flora, 41

Halifax, Nova Scotia, 17
Hamilton, Ontario, 17
Hardin, Garrett, 99
Hegel, 93
Henriprin, Jacques, 104
Housing, 12–16; Report of the Federal Task Force on, 12; federal program on, 13; high rise, 21
Humanae Vitae: papal encyclical on procreation, 146; Canadian Bishop's statement on, 147
Huxley, Julian, 1
Hydrological cycle, 54, 55

Income and fertility values, 123–24
India: food requirements and supply in, 34; projected population growth in, 34; drain on resources in, 6
International corporations, 136
Irrigation, 35, 43, 45

Judeo–Christian ethics and birth control, 146

Knelman, F. H., 139

Leisure, 20
Liebig, Justus, 32, 33, *passim*
London, Ontario, 11

Macpherson, Andrew H., 78
Manicheans, 146
Marine protein, 49, 50–51. *See also* Fishing

Marital fertility, 127, 148
Maritimes, 17
Marx, Karl, 93
Mill, John Stuart, 21
Montreal, Quebec, 10, 16, 23, 25
Morality, a need for a new, 139
Mortality, infant, 81
Myrdal, Gunnar, 68

National Housing Act, 15
National opinion poll: on population, 79; on abortion law, 105
Net reproductive rate, 75; and family size, 118
Nitrates, 47
Nitrogen, 46, 47
Nova Scotia, 80–81

Old Testament and population issues, 92
Oil production, 27
Ontario, 17
Ontario, Lake, 10
Ottawa, Ontario, 17

Paper, manufacture of, 59
Parks, predicted needs for, 21
Pirie, N. W., 41
Pollution: subjective nature of, 4; and levels of consumption, 6; and population density, 6; probe, university surveys, 11, 18; from pulp and paper mills, 18; due to cars, 22; noise, 23, 24; air, 24; individual contribution to, 24; and economic growth, 26; people as, 88, 89
Population growth: as international suicide, 2; history of, 43, 44; limitations on, 58; predictions for Canada, 60; comparative data, 64–65;

and economic growth, 65–66; cost of, 65–67; and net reproductive rate, 73, 74; and voluntary restraints, 76, 130; Interim Report of the National Commission on, 82; ideological influences on, 92–93; Canadian Institute of International Affairs on, 86; and marriage rates, 118; and age at marriage, 147; and social policy, 148–49

Population policy, 109–13, 115; and population optimum, 11, 67–70; political aspects of, 69; goals and objectives of, 71, 76, 97, 98; government, 78–79; professional societies on, 83–85, 87; and technology, 91; and ideology, 91–92, 93; and adaptation to changing conditions, 94; and personal freedom, 96, 98–100; and family planning, 110, 111; and educational programs, 112; and science, 137–38; for Canada, 151

Population size: and sewage, 8; distribution in Canada, 10; and Gross National Product, 26; and food supplies, 31–33; factors in increase of, 61; methods of control, 61; and quality of life, 61; and pressure on resources, 62; demographic considerations, 63–65; and age distribution in Canada, 74–77

Potassium, 46, 47
Potatoes, 41, 44
Potter, Ralph B., Jr., 105, 106, 109
Poultry, selective breeding of, 44
Protestant view on abortion, 105, 106, 109

Protein: resources of the sea, 49; conversion efficiency, 40; yields, comparisons of, 41; sources of, 41; cost of production in land, 41–42; *see* Marine protein, Fishing

Public Health: and use of DDT, 47–48; and irrigation, 45

Quebec City, Quebec, 10, 17

Rasmussen, Knud, 100
Recreation, 20–22
Rice, 44
Roman Catholic. *See* Catholic
Royal Commission on the Status of Women: report on abortion laws, 104

Sacred cow complex, 38
St. Augustine, 146
St. Basil, 146
St. John's, Newfoundland, 17
St. Lawrence River, 10
Sanctions and social goals, 149
Schistosomiasis (Bilharzia), 45, 46
Science Council of Canada, The: 1970 report on population policy, 86
Selective breeding, 44
Sewage, 8, 16–19
Sex education and abortion, 102
Sexual activity, control of, by society, 101
Slums, 13
Snow, C. P., 130
Social goals, conflicting values in, 95–96
Soil erosion, 44
Solid waste, 8, 19, 20
Soybeans, 41, 44
Spengler, Joseph, 100, 122
Status, socio-economic: and reproductive behaviour, 122;

and value of children, 123
Sterilization, 108
Stress: aesthetic 3; physiological, 14; global, 88
Stycos, J. Mayone, 115
Suzuki, David, 55

Technical aid programs, cultural considerations in, 38–39
Technology: and agricultural improvements, 38, 44–45; and fishing, 51, 52, 53; and population problems, 137
Teilhard de Chardin, 92
Tertullian, 1
Third world countries, 38
Time lag and normative behaviour, 127–28
Toronto: population growth in, 13; housing in, 13, 15, 16, 21; sewage treatment in, 17; car population in, 23; carbon monoxide levels in, 24; population density in, 25; spruce-budworm moths in, 48; Zero Population Growth (ZPG) in, 73
Transportation: and urban growth, 14; the need for, 22–25
Trudeau, Pierre Elliott, 28–29, 78–79, 85

Udall, Stewart, 21
United Nations, 2, 97
U. S. National Academy of Sciences: on population size, 89
Urban blight, 15
Urban growth: world predictions, 9; in Canada, 10; implications of, 13–30; causes of, 14
Urbanization, 9–11

Value of children and economic status, 123

Vancouver, B. C., 10, 17

Ward, Barbara, 2
Waste, water. *See* Sewage
Water: consumption of, 18; global supply of, 54–55
Wheat, 41, 46
Windsor, Ontario, 10
Winnipeg, Manitoba, 17

Zero population growth, 72–77; and elimination of unwanted pregnancies, 113–16; and elimination of illegitimate births, 118

LIBRARY OF DAVIDSON COLLEGE

Books on regular loan may be checked out for **two weeks.** Books must be presented at the Circulation Desk in order to be renewed.

A fine is charged after date due.

Special books are subject to special regulations at the discretion of library staff.

DEC 4 '91			